Tell Them Everything

Margaretta D'Arcy

Tell Them Everything

A Sojourn in the Prison of
Her Majesty Queen Elizabeth II
at Ard Macha (Armagh)

Pluto Press

This edition first published in Great Britain by
Pluto Press Limited, Unit 10 Spencer Court,
7 Chalcot Road, London NW1 8LH

Copyright © Margaretta D'Arcy 1981

ISBN 0 86104 349 9

Cover photograph of Mairead Farrell in a cell in Armagh Jail
Cover designed by Michael Mayhew

Typeset by Rowland Phototypesetting Limited,
Bury St Edmunds, Suffolk IP32 6BB
Printed in Great Britain by St Edmundsbury Press,
Bury St Edmunds, Suffolk IP33 3TU

Contents

Author's note / 9
Preface / 11

Part One: The Way In
1. Painful Lessons For a Beginner / 15
2. Custody / 16
3. International Women's Day 1979 / 18
4. Two Steps Forward, One Back / 21
5. Here Was Where I Wanted To Be

Part Two: Inside
6. Correct Procedures / 43
7. First Impressions of A Wing / 48
8. A Wing Routine / 53
9. A Wing Self-Sufficiency / 59
10. Jailors and the Jailed / 61
11. Wise Virgins / 66
12. Getting To Know Them / 70
13. Health / 79
14. Control of Bodies / 83
15. Church / 86
16. Choice of Words / 88
17. Hunger Strike / 95
18. Business In The Yard / 98
19. Culture and Controversy / 103
20. The Last Ditch of the War? / 112

Part Three: Outside
21. Journey's End: Journey's Beginning

The Women on Protest in Armagh Jail / 123
A Short Booklist / 124
Margaretta D'Arcy: A Biographical Note / 125

Author's note

It is not in fact possible to 'tell them everything' because in Britain the intimidating and expensive laws of libel and criminal libel are used by the vested interest of the state as a means of covert censorship. Any truthful book about the oppressive intransigence of the British government's jail policy in the North of Ireland is likely to imperil its publishers and authors. I have regretfully had to accept this.

Margaretta D'Arcy

Preface

Hundreds of women have been jailed in the fight for Irish freedom. In 1798 they were not only jailed but flogged and hanged. Anne Devlin's ordeal in 1803 has gone down in history. There were many women in the prisons in the years following 1916. In 1921 91 of them went on hunger strike in Kilmainham Jail, Dublin. Countess Markievicz's prison letters from this period have been published. Under the Stormont government women were constantly interned; but never in large numbers, and by comparison with the male internees they obtained very little publicity.

Since the early 1970s approximately 120 women have been incarcerated in Armagh—for armed rebellion, or civil disobedience, or merely for being known to hold dissident opinions. In the south of Ireland there are at present two long-term political women prisoners: but there has also been a regular stream of women in and out of the jails for such offences as selling *Spare Rib*, resisting evictions, or demonstrating outside embassies. The legal tactics used against politically active women have included (in one scandalous Dublin case) charges of prostitution which were subsequently dropped. The list is long and growing. For although there are very few 'ordinary' women prisoners in either part of Ireland, the Dublin Government is busy building a new female jail at enormous expense, and, in the North, Armagh Jail is to be turned into a museum and a brand new women's prison erected somewere else.

There has been considerable and acrimonious debate both in Ireland and Britain as to whether the demand for political status by the women in Armagh should be supported as a 'feminist issue'. Why, it has been asked, should the Women's Movement exert itself to assist republican women to obtain allegedly elitist prison conditions, when the Republican Movement itself is male dominated, and has never understood the oppression of women in Irish society? What guarantee is there that the 'New Ireland' will be any different in this respect from the Ireland that produced the notorious 26 County Constitution of 1937? The Constitution includes these grim propositions:

> By her life within the home, woman gives to the state a support without which the common good cannot be achieved . . . The state shall endeavour to ensure that mothers shall not be obliged by economic necessity to engage in labour to the neglect of their duties in the home.

Frankly, until recently, there was no such guarantee. But owing to the influence of *Women Against Imperialism*, and the English-based *Women in Ireland* group, which have been analysing the relationship of women's oppression *in* Ireland to the imperial oppression *of* Ireland, Sinn Fein (in 1980) took the important step of setting up its own Women's Committee. A member of this Committee, Rita O'Hare, herself an ex-political prisoner, stated at a party seminar in Dublin:

> It is only when the Republican Movement recognises the oppression of women, and sees clearly where it comes from—imperialism, social and economic—that the self-lessness, the dedication, and the ultimate sacrifice paid by women volunteers . . . will be truly recognised . . . This year's Sinn Fein Ard Fheis, for the first time ever, is going to be asked to approve a policy document specifically on *Women in the New Ireland* and on Sinn Fein's involvement in the women's struggle until a new Ireland is established. This is a development of major significance, however late we may be in reaching it . . . We cannot wait for the end of British rule, nor can we merely make promises about the things we will do in the new Ireland. We must work, as we must on other social and economic issues, in hammering at the oppression of women now.

Women in the New Ireland was in fact accepted by a surprisingly large majority at the 1980 Ard Fheis (annual party conference of Sinn Fein). In it the party recognises that contraception, family planning and divorce should be available. It also extends the responsibility for the welfare of children to the community as a whole. As expected, older male republicans were against. The document is not a blueprint, by any means, for a feminist utopia; but there is a real radical potential in it. It shows that the Republican Movement now understands that if it leaves women out, there will be no 'New Ireland' for anyone, male or female.

This is a non-dramatic and often rather absurd story of one person who found herself in Armagh Jail for three months during the period of the long-term prisoners' no-wash protest in 1980. The women in Armagh said to me: 'Tell them everything' and this I have tried to do. And since so few books have been written about Irish women's experience as political prisoners over the last two centuries, I felt it essential to put down my own small experience with all its limitations.

Margaretta D'Arcy

Part One: The Way In

1. Painful Lessons For a Beginner

> The struggle by the oppressed for freedom threatens not
> only the oppressor, but also their own oppressed com-
> rades who are fearful of still greater repression. Paulo
> Freire *Pedagogy of the Oppressed*

In the autumn of 1978 I was invited with John Arden to 'do a
double act' at the Queen's University, Belfast, Arts Festival.
This visit, which ought to have been rather agreeable, was in fact
the beginning—without my being aware of it—of a train of
events that was to involve me first with Armagh Jail, then with
Women Against Imperialism and thus as one of the 'Armagh
Eleven', into Armagh Jail again, in the unique circumstances of
the no-wash protest.

I arrived in Belfast a few days before the lecture, a guest of the
Northern Ireland Arts Council. The first big H Block march to
be held in the North had been banned the day after my arrival on
the grounds that it would unduly inflame passions. The following day I went, by invitation, to a poetry reading at the Ulster
Museum. It was pouring with rain and cold as usual, when I
reached the museum. A long buffet table was laid out. It was a
discerning audience, an artistic audience, a caring audience of
sensitive, special people.

The reading began. Paul Muldoon. His first poem was dedicated to a seventeenth-century Spanish painter who had been
banned. No ripple. Then he continued with nature poems about
the Botanic Gardens. Next—Michael Longley: beefy, bearded
and grizzled. He began a poem dedicated to the artist Gerard
Dillon, who had lived in the Falls Road, and whom I had met
several times when I was young and had admired. He was a
courageous gentle person who hated cant. Here, I thought, were
two dead artists being used by two living artists to present an
impression of radical protest against censorship and the

brutality of repression on the Falls Road; did the poets believe that by merely mentioning the names they could avoid all responsibility when the prisoners' families were not allowed to march in the street? It was hypocrisy; it was disgusting. I leant against the wall, took out a red marker and wrote H Block.

Except for the poet's words there was absolute silence at the time. The concentration, the dedication, the reverence to a poet. My marker squeaked; heads turned round; they registered—and they opened their mouths and yelled. I was determined to finish off my 'picture' by putting a frame round it. I was dragged out by the museum attendants, taken downstairs and made to wait for the RUC. The Black Maria arrived, and a young steely-eyed RUC man tipped me in, hoping to break my neck. When I righted myself, he grinned—'How did you like that?' The dream was over, the illusion burst—here I was, staring at the reality of 'Northern Ireland'.

2. Custody

> It just reminds me of a crawling prison in a kind of nightmare, it just extends to include the whole country. Fr Daniel Berrigan

I was taken into the police station, dumped, dragged around like a parcel, laughed at, jeered at, 'Fenian bitch, she's cuckoo'. A policewoman, sodden, stood against the radiator. I wouldn't talk. In and out they came, into my little room, muttering charges under their breath. At about 8 p.m. I was taken to the court-buildings and locked up in a basement cell. There was a wooden bed with a block for my head: a radiator, rusted and lukewarm. Eventually I was given a rubber-covered mattress and grey blankets. Luckily I was wearing a green fur coat, which Eileen Colgan from the Abbey Theatre had given me. I curled up, my heart beating furiously. Did anyone know I was here? I didn't know Belfast, didn't know where I was, and even if I had been told, the address would have meant nothing. My best bet was not to say anything.

The following morning John came, after an overnight journey from London, looking worried. He said they wanted to certify me. He had contacted a lawyer who was opposing this. But it was none the less frightening. They had complete power. If I were put into a mental hospital, they would give me ECT; of that I was sure. They wanted me to talk, and I was not going to. I would not co-operate. The lawyer came, and told me that the charges were serious: three assaults, breach of the peace, incitement to riot, defacing a public monument. I explained that I would not respect the court, nor put in a plea: I would argue about the role of the artist and that was all. He said it would be better if I defended myself alone. I agreed, so I was alone.

I was sent to Armagh to await trial. The reputation of the RUC and the fear inspired by their police stations is so great, it was a relief to go to jail. Plainclothes men drove me down in a private car. I had lost half a stone during the 24 hours in the police station. When I arrived at the prison I refused to answer any questions or co-operate with the doctor. I was taken to A Wing, the remand wing, and Lynn, the Prisoner O.C. for the Provisional IRA company there, came to see me. She accepted me as a republican political prisoner. She arranged for me to share a cell with Ann. We were not to communicate with nor recognise the screws. Everything would be done through Lynn. We shared this cell for a week. There for the first time I heard, through the long nights, of the interrogation methods of the RUC at Castlereagh. The information chilled my blood. Other girls told me what they had been through. All of them were awaiting trial and some had been there two years or more.

Each week for three weeks I would go up to court to make an appearance. Then the case came up. I was able to use my trial to debate the role of the artist in a time of repression. I was fined £10 for each offence. Someone paid my fine, and I left the North. And that was that: or so I thought.

Towards the end of February 1979 I went to Armagh to collect my bag and passport which had been left at the jail, and to stay a few nights.

3. International Women's Day 1979

> She was strongly affected by different girls' fathers and
> brothers being arrested, being interned, for no reason
> at all. That had a big influence on her, I think. She
> went up to visit numerous people in Long Kesh, such
> as boys she knew from Andersontown, of whom there
> were plenty interned. There would hardly have been a
> family she knew that didn't have at least a couple in-
> side, and she went up to Long Kesh regularly to visit
> them. Mrs Farrell, mother of Armagh prisoner
> Mairead Farrell

I stayed with Eleanor, Ann's sister, who became my link with John
when I was inside, and who had visited me, bringing in cigarettes,
books, food. While I was there I rang Mary Enright of the
Relatives' Action Committee, to thank her for having put a greet-
ings message for me in *The Irish News* after my arrest. She told me
about a picket organised by Women Against Imperialism in
Armagh on International Women's Day and invited me to take
part. I said I would, although I knew little of the composition or
purposes of the group.

It was, I discovered, a very small group, not more than fifteen,
made up of two basic sections. First, women (some of them
members of People's Democracy) who had been involved in the
orthodox women's movement in and around Queen's University,
which had tried to bring protestant and catholic women together
on common issues. Inevitably, a split had occurred over the
nature of the Northern Irish state, and the role of the British
Army. Second, women from the Relatives' Action Committee,
mainly married and with small children, and mainly based in
West Belfast, who had had to cope alone with husbands interned or
on the run, and who found that there were specific women's
problems neither fully catered for nor understood by the other
organisations. The fact that there was going to be a picket on that
day was in itself an extraordinary development for the North of
Ireland. It was the first time that women in the North were joining
in the international women's movement against repression and

imperialism, and the first public statement to feminists all over the world that solidarity with the Armagh prisoners and a commitment to oppose British rule were central issues in the struggle for women's liberation

So, on 8 March 1979, a minibus and several cars left Belfast. There were about fifty of us, including two or three men (an American photographer from Glasgow and a couple from People's Democracy and its breakaway group, the Red Republican Party). The women were a mixture—several from People's Democracy, the International Marxist Group, the RAC, Miriam Daly from the Irish Republican Socialist Party. Some of the women had brought their children: Eileen McMullen from the RAC had Dominic; and Mary Enright had Niall, who was two at the time. Never had there been such a large picket at Armagh. The local RAC had held token pickets, but because the centre of Armagh was *black* (that is, unionist), nationalists, stuck outside the town in their estates, were uncomfortable and lacked confidence when protesting inside it. The implication of our audacity escaped me, the outsider. To me it was just another picket.

It was raining as usual—we were muffled in anoraks and plastics. A loud-hailer was produced and a typical North of Ireland protest was set in motion—bawdy republican songs, a calling-out of prisoners' names. The prisoners had been informed of our visit. A white length of material suddenly appeared out of the top window of B Wing. Great cheers. We heard the girls answering back. A genuine warmth and surge of energy united out group. We moved across the road to be closer to our comrades in the jail. Two RUC men stood on the other side of the road, whispering into their walkie-talkies. No other police were evident. A couple of cars turned down the road—and turned back before they reached us. A small group of watchers assembled at the corner. We all spoke through the megaphone. There were last cheers, songs, and good-byes, as we moved away, after an hour, to catch our minibus. The photographer wanted a better view of the new red banner proclaiming *Women Against Imperialism*, and asked us to pose at the main central gate of the jail. We assembled and posed, all smiling and jolly.

Then, as we turned to continue our journey, four RUC jeeps,

appearing out of nowhere, screeched to a halt beside us. Flak jackets and guns. They leapt into the small procession. I saw them grabbing Niall out of the arms of one of the women. Some of us moved forward to help. I was suddenly grasped as if a strong gust of wind had taken hold of the back of my coat. I was lifted into the air and into a waiting jeep, falling on other women who were lying on the floor.

We were driven away to the police station, where a Colombo-type inspector tried to do a funny act. We were lined up at some distance from one another along the corridor. The RUC men and women were lined up on the other side. It was as if we were being arranged by a dancing-master for the opening of the grand ball. One by one we were brought in to see a small miserable specimen of a doctor, sitting behind his desk. A tough, thirtyish, plainclothes policewoman was in attendance.

None of us allowed ourselves to be examined. My heart was going like mad; I was moving in a dream; time was standing still. After being identified, we were brought into a large room with long tables and benches and we waited. Some of the women had stood by their rights. No finger-printing or photos until charged, no answering questions except name and address. Women were dragged and forcibly photographed. They tried to put the pressure on by saying that everyone was going to be released except me, because I was the only one who did not co-operate with them. I had no idea what everyone was saying, as by then we were all shut up in little cubicles. I had not known any of the women before the demonstration: were they going back on their agreed intentions? I didn't care. I was going to carry on regardless. I would only give my name and address. Eventually I was brought back to find everyone together in the large room. One of the RUC kept on looking at me, saying, 'I know your face'. The Colombo character kept on muttering about a woman who had been charged with having gelignite down the Short Strand.

We waited: all of us having been subjected to the same pressure. We felt strong and united. A name was called: its owner was told she could go. She refused, saying, 'All of us, or none of us.' So it went on. We didn't know what had happened to the two men. We were told they had been freed. We didn't believe it. They insisted it was so. They told us we could go. We would be hearing from them. We left in high spirits. The two men were outside, they had been released almost immediately. They looked nervous, particularly the American. He had obeyed them in the beginning, doing and undoing his shoelaces, then he had stopped. It was dark and wet outside, we were freezing. An RAC family took us in, gave us bacon and eggs, tea and bread. We crowded into the little house, in their sitting room, going in and out in relays to eat. The bus driver was there; we departed; handshakes, kisses, cheers; we were off back to Belfast to attend the social put on by Women Against Imperialism.

By six-county standards this was a very minor incident, but even so it produced—as they all do—a new awareness of the strength and vulnerability of the British. The RUC issued statements to the press the next day, saying that we had been released *on bail* (quite untrue), implying that we would all be charged. What with? We had not been charged with anything when we were in the police station. We had not been warned that we had been breaking any particular law. Why had we been released like that and then this falsehood? Were they frightened of the subsequent publicity associating us with International Women's Day? We felt we were in a strong position and were all becoming aware of the significance of the event. A women's conference took place in Trinity College, Dublin, over the weekend. We decided to use the occasion to publicise what had happened and to call on women, north and south, to come back the following month to challenge the right of the RUC to clear us off the streets. If we were to be charged we should stand together as feminists, defending ourselves with perhaps a sympathetic female lawyer to advise us. We were united and we felt strong.

4.   Two Steps Forward, One Back

25 February 1980
I am replying to your letter of 9 February to the Secretary of State. A full investigation of recent events at Armagh

Prison has already been carried out by the Governor of
the Prison. I am satisfied there is no question of any prisoners having been attacked by staff, or having been
denied access to toilets. I can see no justification for
holding any form of Public Enquiry.

Letter from Michael Alison, Minister of State for
Northern Ireland, to Frank Maguire M.P.

We did not realise then how far our unity would be tested over the
next fourteen months nor that we had casually embarked upon a
journey that in retrospect seems to have inevitably led two of us
into the very jail that had been the object of our protest.

The *Belfast Telegraph* published our names and addresses, which
made a couple of the women who worked in the public services very
vulnerable to hostility from their loyalist workmates. Another of
the women had eight children, including a son 'on the blanket'. She
could not put a lot of energy into the trial. One of the young ones
was in the early stages of pregnancy: another one's husband, a
shop-steward, had just lost his campaign against the closure of the
bakery where he worked, so now he was unemployed. The problems
of life in the North of Ireland all seemed to be on show together in
the aftermath of this minor event.

The following September, I was on the way to New York, when
I got a call from Belfast. Eleven summonses had been served (they
did not include the two men). The trial was set for 8 October, but a
solicitor was applying for a postponement. In the event the prosecution postponed the trial until 25 October.

I was already in New York when I got the news. I'd been invited
there by a sympathetic feminist writer, one of the 'White House
Eleven' who had been arrested on an anti-nuclear demonstration in
Washington a little while previously. She and her associates were
shocked by the Armagh charges. News from The North of Ireland
in the American media had been concentrated on the issue of terrorism and its punishment, and there had been no mention of any
peaceful demos. My friend began to organise a petition on our
behalf. Women like Kate Millett and Grace Paley signed.

Public opinion ebbs and flows in the North. By the summer of 1979 the very fact that the men in H Block were still resisting criminal status brought about an increase of confidence among the people, manifested when fifteen thousand marched to Casement Park—the largest demonstration of its kind for years. It made front page news in every British paper, largely because some armed volunteers showed themselves—including a blonde young woman. Young Marie Drumm made a speech from the platform—a significant development. Women Against Imperialism were allowed to march under their own banner. The IRA was now changing its view of the war. It was to be a protracted engagement, Britain was not going to withdraw in the near future, so the tactics had changed: guerrilla warfare would be much more controlled with longer intervals between attacks, and there would be spectacular new operations like the simultaneous bombing of sixteen towns with no loss of life.

A report was leaked to the effect that the IRA could never be militarily defeated, and would indeed increase its technical expertise as the war went on: the British Army was demoralised. This demoralisation seemed confirmed by the simultaneous killings of Lord Mountbatten in Sligo and 18 seasoned soldiers at Warrenpoint. To counteract the apparent failure of the security forces in the field, the new Thatcher government adopted a very hard line on the issue of H Block and Armagh prisoners' demands. The men on the blanket decided that negotiations about their status could not be expected and that they would have to go on hunger strike. They were dissuaded from taking immediate action by the Provo Army Council and instead the RAC called a broad front together to press their demands, without the need for hunger strike. The inaugural meeting was held at the Green Briar social centre in Belfast on 21 October.

The emphasis at the meeting was on the men in H Block. Women Against Imperialism pointed out that there were also protesting women in Armagh Jail. A resolution supporting the Armagh Eleven at our impending trial (now scheduled for 31 October) was passed. One of our members was co-opted onto the new National H Block Committee as a member of the RAC. Another member, put forward to represent Women Against Imperialism, had gathered very few votes—Sinn Fein was taking a cautious view of the new women's group.

Returning to Belfast the night before the trial, I found the original meeting place was changed and our group split between two houses. In one there were two barristers and one solicitor to advise; and, in the other, another two barristers. We were then to assemble all together in the Felons' Club. I had decided not to use a lawyer at all, but to conduct my own case: to be on the offensive, claiming that the prosecution was brought largely due to the RUC's need to notch up convictions and overtime. (We had been arrested after 3 p.m., and by then the police were being paid overtime). The lawyers advised the women to plead guilty—otherwise they would get heavy sentences. They were treating the cases as ordinary criminal ones in an ordinary criminal situation. Some of the women began to feel distressed, so we went to see another barrister, but the consultation with her was equally inconclusive.

By this time it was late, and we went to the club. The meeting between the other women and the lawyers had not taken place. There were several women at the club who were not in the Armagh Eleven, but were in Women Against Imperialism. There were very unpleasant scenes, largely because they had been hanging around a long time waiting for us. One woman, who had been working with a nationalist solicitor during the summer, said his advice was that we should recognise the court. I said I couldn't do that. Women attacked me for selfishness. It seemed that I, the outsider, was to be treated by them as a scapegoat for all the confusion. All their fears and the pressures they were under were thrust on me. I said I would not be emotionally blackmailed. We had not worked out our case. The barristers were now taking over. I was not dealing with them. I had chosen an independent course and they couldn't interfere with my rights. We broke up in confusion. Specially-printed T-shirts, 'Political Status for Armagh Women Prisoners', were given to us to wear in court. We made no other plans.

The following morning the sun was shining brightly. We had hired a coach. We were all in fine form—united again. We sang and made up songs. Through the singing we became stronger and the fears of the previous night disappeared. There were some supporters with us in the coach, which added to our confidence. The court—a freshly-painted early nineteenth-century building— was very beautiful. Inside were scores of RUC men and women. A special court had been booked. The barristers were there with their briefs. They had got photos from the police and were examining them. We had been expecting the trial to go on for several days. We were told that the court was booked only for one. Would it all be over in one day? What about witnesses who were only available the next day? We filed in—we did not stand up. We all wore our T-shirts. One of the barristers indicated that I should sit nearer to them as I was conducting my own case. Basil McIvor was the magistrate—an ex-Minister for Education under Brian Faulkner— a long-faced northerner with mild manners. He did not bat an eyelid when we remained seated. He asked me if I was comfortable, if I'd seen the evidence of the photos. He asked the barrister to hand them to me. He appeared very interested in the feminist song we had sung, asking where the melodies had come from: he did not know about International Women's Day. Looked intent when told about it. Altogether a leisurely beginning.

The other women now began to relax and move closer to the front to hear better. The barristers were brilliant at knocking holes in the Inspector's evidence. 'A movie camera had been used—no, it couldn't be produced because it hadn't been working—yes, he had written his notes up at a later date.' There had been only two RUC officers at the picket to begin with because the others were needed for border control. They had to ring up for reinforcements—yes, bawdy songs had been sung, they were usual at these demos. Yes, he had been worried about a small group of people assembled at the corner, who had said, 'Get this scum out of our town'. He was worried in case violence would break out: and so on. The barristers were doing a good job and were pleased with themselves. I had to follow this brilliant cross-examination. I felt more and more ner- vous as the minutes ticked by. I was praying that by four o'clock the court would be adjourned.

The atmosphere was one of civilised debate and lenient paternalism. I stood up and said, 'As someone from the 26 Counties I would like to know how much this court is costing. It is obvious that the two witnesses, the doctor and the Inspector, are lying.

Why don't we just dismiss the case and have no more nonsense?' McIvor's face changed as rapidly as Dr Jekyll into Mr Hyde. He thumped, 'How dare you!' I then examined the Inspector. What time did he come on duty for overtime and was he on overtime now? Mr McIvor dismissed the court, stormed out—I shouted a few slogans to his retreating back. There was uproar. The RUC closed in on me, tried to arrest me. Eilis came forward and said, 'Release her arm'. One of the young male lawyers began shouting at me, 'Fuck off'. The facade was broken, all that was left was the shattered illusion of democracy in the North of Ireland. I was not popular with anyone.

Late that night, we had a meeting. It was agreed that the fantasy of court procedure and justice had indeed taken hold of everyone. We were once again all women together, recognising that our appalling behaviour of the night before had been due to our nerves being at stretching point. One section had begun drinking too early, the other group had arrived sober just before closing-time. We assured ourselves that we now knew all the tricks of the courts and the barristers. We would take control of our own trial. The next time, 2 January, I would conduct my case first. I would write out the questions that I intended to ask and give them to the lawyers who would thus be prepared. I would needle and the lawyers would then pick up the pieces. I had no legal knowledge and I would not ask legal questions pertaining to the case. Nor would I ask feminist questions as McIvor would obviously love to lead me down a cul-de-sac, and anyway we had never, as a group, discussed feminism.

The following morning, the Belfast newspapers gave good coverage to the case: how we all wore T-shirts, the farce of the movie camera, etc. The *Republican News* however was not interested. Women had not yet asserted their own identity. Nonetheless we felt confident that we were slowly establishing ourselves as a women's anti-imperialist group; despite internal differences we were determined to maintain our collective cohesion.

The postponement of the trial till January gave us a breathing space to mobilise support from women's movements abroad. A picket had been put outside the British Consulate in New York. In

London, Women-in-Entertainment were going to have an all-women show at the Ritzy, Brixton, at the end of April. Everywhere women's groups showed a willingness to involve themselves in the trial of the Armagh Eleven.

I found it a heavy personal strain to have to make the London-Stranraer-Belfast journey repeatedly, in the midst of my ordinary professional and domestic life. I had already been arrested under the Prevention of Terrorism Act at Stranraer in January when I was returning to Armagh. When you are released after these short harassment-arrests the relief is so great that you are quite amazed at the turmoil created inside yourself at the time—the panic, the isolation, the feeling of being obliterated from the world. You are in a nervous state anyway on such a trip. On the long night's journey from Euston, who is watching whom? The train is always half-empty, you lie drowsy in an empty carriage. Would some drunk loyalist come and attack? What if there is a crash as we hurtle through the dark, slugging our way through the wilderness of Scotland? Getting out at 5.30 a.m., cold, damp, you wait in line for the security control. How to go through as if it is the most natural act in the world? To be too cocky makes you conspicuous; too nervous, a beady eye will take note. So you have to find an even balance to face the open smiling face of the police: smile returned, smile, candid eye to candid eye. Women officials seem to be the most efficient. Their fingers probe the luggage, no smile: duty, responsibility. A bit of paper comes out. She reads, then goes over to a man for a consultation. They look. Other passengers pretend not to notice, all go through. 'Come this way please.' You enter into a broom-bucket-and-mop cupboard. No windows, a TV monitor high on the wall. You sit down, a policewoman sits. Say nothing. The door opens, a male constable. 'Would you come down to the police station?' 'Why?' They are always reluctant to say why. You have to push them to come out about the Prevention of Terrorism Act. Private car outside in the yard. In you go and are driven off—god knows where.

No-one knows you, no-one has seen you—no good to leave a bit of paper with 'help' written on it. You cannot ring up anyone. Whom would you ring, in Stranraer? Left alone in an interrogation room, a chair, a table, UVF, UDA, initials on the wall—names,

Mary, John, Thomas. Stare out of the window, get closer to the radiator, three cigarettes left, one match, lean on the radiator. Footsteps, whispering, keys jangling, make no noise. A head pops in—a head goes out. After five hours, a pleasant Scots Inspector comes in. 'You may go.' Your bag is given to you. You're late, the boat has gone. Go back to the buffet. Suspicious eyes. Do they know? Control the trembling of your hand. Crouch over a newspaper. Still the same routine again.

30 December. Back again to Northern Ireland. A meeting is being held in a house in Suffolk, a working-class ghetto of Belfast. Slogans on the flats: 'don't be an armchair republican', 'join your unit', 'victory to the blanket men', 'up the Provos', 'up the INLA'. At the house, all was chaos. Mary has to hire a lorry for the first national Smash H Block march the following day. Loud-hailers, equipment, have to be hired. Groups of feminists seem to be coming from all parts of the United Kingdom. Feminists from Dublin: who is to meet them? A meeting of the lawyers has been arranged. Sue's getting in new T-shirts for all of us, but what about the supporters? Will the coach be large enough? Small enough? Who will look after the kids? What about witnesses? What about the press? Travel-exhausted women come in. It is New Year's Eve—the equivalent in the North to Christmas Day in England. There are no buses from the station and they have had to walk. We, the outsiders, just sit holding cups of tea in our cold hands.

1 January. A slow beginning, hanging around waiting for the lawyers. Una was now seven months pregnant. Some of the 'Eleven' couldn't be there. We agreed it was unlikely that McIvor would have any of us sent down for contempt of court—there were too many foreign women present. We all went on the march—the usual bitchings about lack of militancy in the Smash H Block Committee, because they didn't want confrontations between the British Army and the youth. Pat Arrowsmith gave a rousing speech, to the amusement of the young women in the crowd. 'She looks like a Brit, and talks like a Brit, but she isn't saying things a Brit would.' Warm applause for Pat.

The next morning was clear and crisp—a pink sunrise on the black mountains. Once again farewell to the children. We hang around Dunville Park, popping in and out of the Sinn Fein Centre to keep warm. Relatives are waiting for the shabby minibus to take them to the Kesh. Piles of clothes and parcels—all is routine, paced out. Nobody can ever fluster Sinn Fein workers, they are unflappable. Today we have a good relationship with Sinn Fein. Our methods might be different but there is a comradeship. We buy peppermints and cigarettes from the little shop next door. Where is the coach? It is 9 o'clock, where is everybody? Once again we are on our way to Armagh singing the 'women's army' song.

Our nervousness is gone. The British Army have put up a roadblock outside Armagh. We are stopped. Soldiers climb onto the bus; tension; no-one speaks. Should we leave the bus, when a pipsqueak officer tells us to? We say no. He says we can stay there all day. We say we have to be at Armagh Court for 11 o'clock. He says, 'Bugger the court.' We say he is now defining the Army as being above the law. Is he aware of that? He says that he doesn't give a damn. We would like to take his number but don't know what regiment he is in and can't see any insignia. We sit. Someone gets up and goes out. We all go. But we refuse to give more than our names and addresses. We sing outside and clap our hands. There was really nothing else to do but leave the bus. Half a dozen male and female soldiers, guns pointed. The visitors are shocked. We continue singing. After an hour we are allowed back on, we are late, we compose another verse:

> The British Army blocked our way
> On the way to court today
> What will Basil McIvor say
> When the women's army is late?'

A lot of our supporters are waiting outside when we arrive. They are being searched one by one. We are not allowed to enter: we hang around. The pipsqueak officer has suddenly popped up again with his unit, carrying cameras this time. Marie pretends to do a strip-dance and then a belly-dance. We all laugh, clap, and do the can-can, bawling our songs out. We sing loudly as we enter the building, our voices soaring to the ceiling. Surprisingly, tea is being served: the RUC is in good humour because of our good humour. There's a delay; then upstairs to consult the barristers.

They say the prosecuting barrister is ill—there will be no trial today. We huddle together to work out our next move. We want no postponement. We will stay in court until we are heard. We will not come back another day. No more postponed trials . . . The barristers will be dismissed once McIvor announces the new date. The barristers cannot say 'We will not come back'; so we have to be rid of them before *we* can say it. We are huddled in court—whispering. I am clutching my 'evidence', the Human Rights Charter, the Bennett Report and the Pope's speech at Drogheda.

McIvor comes in. I am prodded to ask him about the return of the banner taken from us when we were arrested. I stand up. 'Mr McIvor,' I say. He glares. 'Address me by my proper name: Your Honour.' I change my tone, I am all concerned, I talk with a soothing voice. 'Mr McIvor,' I say, 'surely you cannot expect me to'—I look around at all the women—'to call you, Your *Honour*?' He explodes, the lawyer gets up: 'Your Honour, can we have the banner back?' 'No!'

Then McIvor announces that there will have to be a postponement till April. I get up and say it is unacceptable to me. 'Try us now, or dismiss the charges.' He ignores me. He looks at the barristers, who slowly, each in turn, get up and say: 'My client has at this moment dismissed me.' McIvor looks incredulous: 'At this moment?' He can hardly believe his ears. For a moment he says nothing. 'But that is impossible'. 'It's true,' they say. We all sit, McIvor looks at us in silence. We begin singing and clapping our hands, getting up and dancing. He storms out.

An elderly policeman says, 'Dismiss the court.' He then conducts the singing. After a bit we leave, to sing songs of solidarity outside the jail and to call out the names of the prisoners of war inside. They answered us back and there we left them. Locked up in B Wing for 21 hours. No food parcels. Brave fighters for Irish freedom. They would stay there for ever if we didn't get them out. It ought to be easy—all we had to do was be transformed into the Incredible Hulk and with one leap we could tear the walls down. We would be back. No Army nor RUC visible. In fact, as a result of our arrest last year, women were now able to demonstrate there undisturbed.

But it had become clear that we were never going to be allowed to stand up in court and explain why we had been demonstrating in the first place!

Back in West Belfast, in the Lake Glen Hotel, we had another meeting. Would we gain anything by turning up again or were they wearing us down? We couldn't keep asking for observers to each postponement, and obviously as long as we brought supporters with us they would give us no trial. Also our emphasis appeared to be shifting, concentrating more on our trial than on the conditions of the women in the jail. The arguments went back and forth. Were we romantic Provos to not want any more truck with the courts? The republican women said that they had gone along so far with the legal process, now they were having no more of it. It was not worth the concerted energy involved. Anyway, the barristers had been dismissed. They had not been able to answer our most relevant questions: what fines would be imposed? What would happen if they were not paid? Could we be given prison sentences? No-one in the North of Ireland knows. It's all arbitrary. Were we going to be hounded for the rest of our lives? We decided to work for a massive turnout on 8 March, International Women's Day. The British women would go back to their groups and mobilise. Those in Belfast would organise an international inquiry into the conditions of the women in jail. It had been a comedy turn while it lasted. Women were now aware of us. Gains had been made. The Republican Movement was taking note at last of the importance of the women's question and of the women in Armagh Jail. Sinn Fein had called for a women's conference for its members. But for Women Against Imperialism it was only one part of the struggle. The newspapers still had to be got out, and a women's centre set up in hard-pressed West Belfast.

I left for America, at the invitation of the War Resisters' League and the anti-nuclear movement associated with it, to present a thirty-hour event of my plays about Ireland in Washington Square Church, New York. It was there I was told of the riot in Armagh Jail on 7 February. Away from Belfast it was impossible to get up-to-date news. I scanned the British press—a report of a remark by Cardinal O Fiaich about 'H Block conditions' inside Armagh—male prison officers on the wing—prisoners beaten—

Father Murray not allowed to visit the girls. I could not believe that
the British would allow this to happen inside a women's jail. I still
didn't really believe that on 9 April McIvor would send us down: it
would be too much to our advantage. The British propaganda had
insisted that only terrorist women were jailed. If ten feminists were
to go in, wouldn't it be an intolerable embarrassment? But another
inner voice whispered: 'No-one really gives a damn for northern
Irish people, it's just been going on too long, it's all so confusing.'
It seemed so insoluble, anything could happen.

International Women's Day at Armagh had been a great success.
The *Republican News* had a whole centre-page—500 women had
marched. Women had come from everywhere. I'd given some
readings at the People's Voice Café on that day, and women there
had reached out to the women in the North of Ireland. We were
sure at Washington Square Church that the British government
would be too intelligent to sentence us to jail. We read in the
papers that small fines had been imposed on us. I didn't think they
would be bothered to collect the fines, so I returned to London, on
my way back to Galway.

5.   Here Was Where I Wanted To Be

> Listen to the valleys,
> Its mountains and its dales,
> Its lament for its dead,
> And those held in British gaols.
>
> Time has proven no friends of the Irish,
> Still they are tortured and killed,
> But yet, amidst the ruin of destruction,
> The ideals, the dreams, still live.
>
> Erin speaks softly,
> But firmly in her voice.
> Whispers in the night,
> Flowing gently in the wind.
>
> Verses from Bernie Boyle (Armagh prisoner) *The Voice of Erin*

I had been in London only one day when I received a phone-call from Belfast. The first of the Armagh Eleven had been picked up for non-payment of her fine, and was now in Armagh jail. She was Ann-Marie, a single parent with four children. The caller did not know if any warrant had yet been issued for me, but she told me that I had been sentenced to six months if my fine was not paid, and of course I had not paid it.

One of the Eleven, a young woman from Belfast who was studying in England, decided she would pay her fine: was I going to do the same? Some feminists in London were advising us all to pay the fines; and that the money that had been collected at the Women-in-Entertainment Benefit should be used to do so. But that money had been donated as a gesture of solidarity to the prisoners of war inside the jail for their relatives to spend on anything they wanted, or for the upkeep of the children of the Armagh Eleven while their mothers were in prison. Fortunately others were as worried by this as I was, and the money in the end went where it had been intended to go.

I began to feel more than a little paranoid. Then, when I was about to start for Belfast—I felt I must be there together with the other women for as long as I was still free—I had another call to say that there was now a warrant out for me. How seriously was I to take this warrant? Were we such a threat to the Northern Ireland Office that they were going to grab us wherever they could? They certainly could arrest me anywhere in England or Scotland. Or was it just routine—one's name coming up on the computer because it happened to be on a list of petty crimes along with hundreds of others? Torn between 'on the run' and 'just routine', I travelled once more to Belfast.

I wasn't even asked for an identity document this time: and I arrived in the city, on Friday 9 May, just in time for the press conference to publicise Ann-Marie's case, and to publicise the fact that warrants had now been issued for some of us. By this time Armagh Solidarity groups had been formed in Belfast and in Dublin, which to my relief had unanimously decided to support the Armagh Eleven's refusal to pay the fines and to go to jail instead.

In fact, five out of the eleven had decided they would pay; so six of us were going inside. I then learned that I was going in for only four months, not six as I had originally been told. Three of us had been singled out by the court as 'leaders', presumably because we were not from the North of Ireland. The world could then be persuaded that we were 'outside agitators' and northern public opinion would lose interest in us.

Ann-Marie's domestic problems had been solved. Two of her children were now with their father in Dublin and two in Belfast. Ann-Marie had not been told—she assumed that they were all in Belfast. That afternoon there was a call from Armagh Jail saying that Ann-Marie's fine had been paid and she was on her way home. Who had paid? Was it the Brits? Or someone else who wanted to discredit Women Against Imperialism? It turned out to be Ann-Marie's 73-year-old mother-in-law, who, without telling anyone, had gone down to Armagh that very day, in the heatwave, had wandered around the police stations trying to find out how to pay it and had returned home in triumph.

The mother-in-law disapproved of her daughter-in-law, so had sprung into action with a high moral tone. This whole non-payment-of-the-fine thing was ridiculous, she said, we were all filth—she spat the words out at us. There was too much suffering in the North of Ireland, too many grandiose gestures and what about her grandchildren? The irony of the situation could not escape me. The old woman was exerting her 'right to choose'. The 'eternal female' had risen from the ashes and with one clean swoop was destroying everything that Women Against Imperialism stood for. Years of subjection had built up a foaming resentment inside her: and she did not want anything better for her daughters. 'For the sake of the children'—why had she waited for a whole week, until the children were all settled? She must have felt that her generation was no longer in control. On this occasion she couldn't be argued with. She stood firm, 'filth, filth' she screamed. What about Ann-Marie, pale, worked up? We found her in her council house where we gathered to give her support. She didn't know what had hit her. When the Governor had told her that her fine was paid, she couldn't believe him. 'Where is the receipt?' she kept on asking. 'My dear,' he said, 'you are the receipt.'

The whole thing was becoming absurd. The hard men in the Republican Movement would think she couldn't take it. But that was the least of her worries. More important was how to get her children back from her separated husband. I don't know why: but all the events in the North of Ireland seem to have heavy elements of knockabout farce.

On Sunday May 11 we all went to Dublin to a women's conference, held in Trinity College to support Ann-Marie and the rest of the Armagh Eleven. We arrived to be told that Sue would pay her own fine and that they thoroughly disapproved of any of us going to jail. They thought we might escalate the protest by going on hunger strike which would only make the situation worse! Liz and I were outsiders anyway and it should be local women who went into jail. They would 'support us externally' and that was that. To be faced by a Trinity College undergraduate behaving like a fault-finding mother-superior was more than I could stand. Why was there this sudden switch? We should have had a meeting among ourselves and Sue should have told us herself about paying the fine. But no meeting—it was all decided. We were seething. I felt I was going mad. No-one said a word to Ann-Marie.

In the afternoon the main meeting took place. Rose McAllister, an ex-Armagh prisoner, spoke very effectively as usual, detached and sharp. There was considerable support from the more republican members of the audience for our decision to go to jail. Privately, I wondered if I would ever get there. Yet I had to get myself into that prison. If necessary, I would go in without external support and I would not let my 'supporters' change my decision for me. As a writer committed to the integrity of the written word, I felt we had raised the expectations of the young women in Armagh (who were in there for ten to twenty years and many of them firmly maintaining their innocence); and they were all expecting us to come and join them. If we failed in our undertaking, they would think we had been manipulating the situation for our own politics. Besides, if I now determinedly refused to pay the British government for the privilege of speaking the truth during a peaceful protest, and kept on refusing till they sent me to jail, at least a few people still concerned for civil liberties might be perturbed at the implications.

The difference in approach between People's Democracy and the Republican Movement was very marked, and not helpful. PD did not want their members in Women Against Imperialism to go to jail, because they would gain too much kudos and undue advantage in the party afterwards. PD women were very conscientious workers, but within WAI were few in number compared to the women from Sinn Fein and their absence in prison might afford Sinn Fein too much preponderance within WAI. Any influence PD had with the Republican Movement and the Smash H Block Committee would be undermined if non-PD members of WAI went into jail while PD members paid fines . . .

These issues were never discussed. No-one ever tried to explain why pressure was put on us to break our word and pay the fines. There was one other possible motive—ordinary human fear. To go into jail as an advocate of international socialist feminism without being a member—or wholehearted supporter—of the IRA, meant that we would be in a minority among the other prisoners. How would they treat us? And what about women personally liberated through lesbianism, how would they retain their independence in such a catholic-conservative environment? Was it a fear primarily of the other prisoners; or simply that the women were unable to face the atrocity of the no-wash protest? I shall never know: it was never discussed.

Instead, high-falutin marxist jargon was bandied back and forward: 'idealism', 'petit bourgeois', 'individualism', 'martyrdom', etc. No-one in that hall knew exactly who the Armagh Eleven were. The women who had decided to pay the fines were not identified to the conference. I was going to jail, and yet I couldn't tell anyone. The talk was that 'the Armagh Eleven have decided this or that . . .' The Armagh Eleven had become as distanced, as abstract as any other cause set up by the male left-wing groups. A more personal approach, a sisterly identification, were badly needed, and were lacking. I was alone and must take the consequences.

We were not a happy, united, Women Against Imperialism the night before going back to Belfast. Ann-Marie still had to collect her children. We had proved so disunited in our anti-imperialism, we had all rallied round Ann-Marie's personal struggle against her ex-husband; and we decided we were going to support her 'right to look after her own'.

We arrived at a house outside Dublin at about 9 p.m. I can only describe what ensued as a surrealist happening. The plan was simple: knock on the door, the door opens, march in and collect the children, then leave. In fact we waited outside while voices were raised in the house, cries and sobbings. Windows began opening in this quiet cul-de-sac, nosey neighbours' heads materialised at the windows, mysterious cars began to appear in the street; we scramble in and out of the coach, knock at the door, peer in the letter-box. Shadows behind the curtains of the room where Ann-Marie had gone; raised fists, sudden movements: physical force? Time was running out; we were supposed to collect everyone else at the pub at 10.30, it was 10.30 already. Ann-Marie came out of the house, sobbing. We all felt humiliated. We retreated, without the children.

I hung around Belfast Monday and Tuesday in a kind of limbo. I was fed up, couldn't talk to anyone. I hoped to God I would be picked up by the RUC. I was going like a yo-yo in and out of the security gates in the middle of the city, trying to get myself questioned and thus recognised. Come what may, I would be in jail by Wednesday. I would deliver myself either alone on Wednesday morning or at six in the evening with supporters.

In fact, when I sat down to look coolly at the position of the Armagh Eleven, it was not really so bad. Two had had their fines paid by their families, three were paying their own fines, one was not coming up from the 26 Counties, one had paid her fine because all along she said that she would. That left four of us. Even four of us in jail would be a respectable proportion. But out of that four, one had just had a baby and was now suffering from a cyst on the vagina and one had a problem with her daughter who had been caught shop-lifting. The mother was having to go to the juvenile court to explain the family circumstances. That still left two. There was no reason why WAI couldn't issue a statement saying that we were going in *on behalf* of the Armagh Eleven.

Tuesday night's meeting was not going to be smooth. Before it took place I bumped into Liz in the Rock Bar across the road. She said she was going to give herself up whatever happened at the meeting, she couldn't stand any more, she was a nervous wreck.

The Armagh Solidarity group (including WAI) met first. On the agenda were the forthcoming street demonstrations—a roadblock outside Andersonstown police station, and a big city-centre demo for the next Saturday. Sinn Fein was very wary about the dangers of alienating support if the road was blocked at 5 o'clock. A compromise was worked out. When we were asked if any more of us were going into jail, one of the Women Against Imperialism said it hadn't been decided. It would be discussed later on that evening when WAI had its own meeting. I said there was nothing to decide. I was giving myself up on the Wednesday. The only thing to be discussed was whether I was going alone or getting support. That was an ultimatum. Someone then asked whether WAI regarded me as a member of the group. A couple of them said that that was up to me. I said I didn't mind. One of them snapped back, if I was a member I was to abide by the rules. I said that to talk as if there were a manifesto or rule-book for Women Against Imperialism when there wasn't any was politically ominous. Someone said that the remark had not been intended. I said I would give myself up either at 10 in the morning or 6 in the evening. Then we held our own WAI meeting. First, a Dutchwoman's visit to Belfast to help set up a women's centre was discussed. This took a long time. I thought there was some stalling going on. I raised once again the question of my giving myself up. Sue hummed and hawed; then Liz said, 'What about me?'

A member said it had already been decided at the last meeting, that those who wanted to go to jail should do so. Still Sue went on, begging, pleading, that we should not give ourselves up—even turning her face away to hide her tears. What was going on? And why was everyone so helpless to stop this slow torture of Liz and myself? I couldn't believe it was really happening. There was no discussion about who was to write to us, about a statement to give the press: but just on and on over the same ground. Only at the last minute was it finally decided that there should be a support-group to see me off and that I should turn myself in, to the RUC at 6 o'clock the next evening. The meeting finished five minutes before closing time. We raced across to the Felons' Club, only to be told that 'on orders from above', no-one from Women Against Imperialism was to be served. We hung around arguing, a fragmented group, my làst night of freedom spent haranguing on the pavement whilst the Brits in their Saracens zoomed up and down.

I had to prepare my mind for going in. There was a real possibility that I would be totally isolated in the jail. Why should the women republican prisoners receive me with loving arms when they had been led to believe that eleven of us were coming in? I tried to fasten my mind on positive things. I remembered Countess Markievicz and Rosa Luxemburg's prison letters and the importance to them of flowers and insects. I decided I would smuggle in seeds on my shoes, lettuce and onion seeds, and grow them in my shit. One little shoot would give me something to concentrate on. There would be no books, no intellectual stimulus of any kind, and no support from outside. I was sure that I would crack. I had embarked on the journey out of a genuine conviction that accepting criminalisation at no matter how trivial a level would be to fall in with the British plan of making criminals of all nationalists if they resisted or dissented in any way. With a single change of the law a large section of the population, without realising it, without coercion, had been induced actively to assist in its own destruction. I could not go along with this.

One becomes very conscious of the poverty when one looks for and cannot find an ordinary commodity such as seeds. No-one in Belfast seemed to grow anything, and yet this was May, the bedding time. All Wednesday I searched the shops. In the end I managed to obtain one packet each of lettuce and onion seeds. I scattered them in my shoes and in the crevices of my clothes, and set out. Yet another worry: was there really a warrant prepared for me? This uncertainty invested my going in with an air of unreality. No-one delivers themselves up in the North of Ireland. The whole episode appeared ridiculous.

Anyway, I rang the barracks at 5 p.m. asking them if there was a warrant out for me about the fine. Was it due? It was. I asked how many days it was overdue and why it had not been served. Well, they didn't like being too hard on people (this was the RUC). I had a problem, I told them: what about the value of the Irish Punt? I would have to pay in Irish money. Well, they said, couldn't I wait till tomorrow, go to the bank and then bring the money to the barracks in English pounds? No, I said, because bank charges would be incurred. He would have to appreciate my point of view. Being fined was bad enough but then having to pay bank charges . . . Well, in the end it was decided that I would go down to the police station and clear it all up. What time could I be expected? About 6 p.m., I said. That was that.

Six o'clock, made my way downtown, a group of women and men were assembled at the agreed meeting-place. The banner was there, a child was despatched to buy me my last packet of cigarettes, and we were off singing 'The Women's Army' as we weaved our way down the Whiterock Road to the Fort. We stopped outside, my photo was taken for sympathetic papers, then we knocked. A soldier shouted down, 'What do you want?' 'We want to make a complaint' 'What, all of you?' 'Yes, all of us.' We waited while the message was rung through, then the great door was opened and in we marched. The yard was full of Saracens. Stretched out on one of them wearing a bikini was Miss United Kingdom, posing for pin-ups. The original small police station was still standing in the middle of all this. We crowded into the waiting-room. There were ordinary notices on the wall about rabies, etc. The Inspector came out.

I voiced my complaint about my warrant not having been served, it showed a lack of efficiency, a lack of commitment to the Tory government, an insult to Mrs Thatcher and her housekeeping policy, a fundamental lack of patriotism, an undermining of the unionist loyalty to the crown. Where was my warrant? He said, 'Are you going to pay the fine?' I said, 'No,' and we all said, 'We are not moving until it is served.' He went back, and we saw him through the window making phone-calls. We sang songs, clapped our hands. After quite a long delay, he returned and said, 'You will get what your hearts desire.' We shouted, 'What! So soon? A 32-county small-farmers' and workers' socialist republic, amnesty for all prisoners?' He said drily, 'No, not that yet. Come this way.' The others stayed outside singing.

My warrant was produced and to my amazement it turned out that my sentence was for only 3 months. I had been given 3 months on one charge and 2 months on the other, to run concurrently. I didn't believe it at first, I was sure they had changed it. With many compliments about my 'send-off' (The RUC are really quite extra-ordinary), I was taken away to the court-house cells, to spend the night there. From now on time stood still.

I asked no questions about my fate: the state had taken me over to do with what they would. I slept heavily in the very same cell I had occupied 18 months before. The next morning I was driving down the motorway in a red Cortina car, with two plainclothes-men in front, a plainclothes-woman beside me, and the radio playing 'Pretty Baby'. To anyone not familiar with car registrations we would have seemed a foursome going out to the country on this glorious, warm, sunny day. I leaned back, avoiding contact with the anaemic policewoman in her body-coloured stockings, green skirt and cardigan. We soon arrived at Armagh, I had 91 days left to serve, and here was where I wanted to be.

Part Two: Inside

6. Correct Procedures

> Of course I hate the suffering you are all going through
> and I would take that away if I could . . . I'm not being
> morbid but sometimes we achieve more by death than we
> could ever hope to living. . . . We dedicated our lives to
> a cause that is supremely more important than they were.
> Sometimes I feel very selfish because it is easy for us but
> you are the ones who'll experience the heart-ache. Marion
> Price on hunger strike in a letter to her mother, 1974.

Armagh, May 15: a regency jail in the middle of an eighteenth
century town. Since my previous visit new reinforcement had been
added to the external fortifications, to protect emerging warders
from sudden attacks. The car drives up, the bell is rung, a certain
amount of nervousness as we wait for the gate to be opened. We
enter: more waiting around, jailors with keys unlocking and locking bolts, we drive into the courtyard. I wait for the car door to be
opened for me. The RUC woman and a jailor escort me through the
ground floor and what seems to be the boiler room. I'm taken into
an office, my particulars are noted down. I give only my name and
address. The screws seem to remember me. They are friendly. I
give limited co-operation as I do not want them to have any excuse
for not sending me to A Wing. They could put me in the hospital
wing saying I was mentally exhausted or something like that.

The dark one said, 'It's not really as bad as what they say, you
know, they do get sanitary towels,' looking at me plaintively. I ask
her why she was condoning the atrocities by working there. She
said, 'If we withdrew our labour who will feed them?' I said that if
there was general disgust at the treatment of the women, why
didn't she make representations within the prison officers' union?
In January there had been rumours that the union was going to take
some initiative. She said the sympathetic ones were too few.

I didn't think any northerner would ever waste the energy I was putting forward to explain the possibility of a new Ireland, once the partition and the partition-created political parties were removed. But then there are very few people from the 26 Counties in jail in the North of Ireland; and in all probability I was the only one that the screws here had ever had the opportunity of meeting. In a way I was their bogey, the reason for their fear, so in turn I had to represent the true virtues of the 26 Counties: reasonable, enlightened, compassionate, non-sectarian.

While I was taking the compulsory bath, I overheard one of them saying, 'Well at least she's different, it makes a change.' Not quite what I had expected, no overnight conversion . . .

The question as to whether or no I should co-operate in a dignified way with the preliminaries of entry into the jail—i.e. the stripping and the bath—had not been discussed before I gave myself up. I had to be very careful not to outdo the militancy of the other prisoners. I did not come from the North: there was no way I could act as though I were from the oppressed minority of the ghettos. I had for example never personally experienced the savagery of the loyalists and the screws knew this. I was there because I object in principle to the British presence in the six Counties, the subjugation of the minority, and the treatment of the prisoners.

As far as I knew there was no campaign against taking the routine bath on admission—I did not want to be a freak. You don't have to be examined naked—the screws discreetly look over a sheet you wrap round yourself for scars and marks. I preferred not to find out what would have happened had I refused. I was conscious of the double standard here, but I was not sure of my ground, so I went along. On dressing I was told I couldn't wear my black trousers. I was amazed, these were the same trousers that I'd worn before, and there had been no objection. They said 'new rules', and I remembered that it was the wearing of the black 'uniform' that ostensibly had been the reason for the prison officers' riot of 7 February. I said that I had not been informed about these new rules. It was up to the Governor to inform the RUC so I could have the opportunity of arriving in different clothes. They said, 'We could give you other clothes to wear.' I said, 'No, I have a right to wear my own clothes.' I was on solid ground here, no-one could make me wear prison clothes. They stood around helpless, what were they to do?

I suggested they rang my friends in Belfast to send down new clothing. They said no. I said that, in that case, I should have to wear what I had on: a red cotton Indian shirt and my knickers. They said that I couldn't go on the wing looking like that. What was to be done? It was a problem. Then Big Susie said, 'We'll ask Mairead.' (Mairead is the prisoner appointed by the IRA from the outside to be OC of republican prisoners in A wing. Inside the jail—whatever the British Government propaganda—the prisoners are recognised as IRA volunteers and their officer is accepted as their spokesperson). So a screw was despatched to A Wing—I wondered what she would look like when she returned. She looked pretty much the same. Mairead had told her to go to the remand centre in B Wing and ask the republican OC there (Jennifer) for some clothes. A screw was despatched to Jennifer. I was sitting in my cubicle while they all waited with bated breath. What would happen if Jennifer didn't send the clothes? I was feeling quite cheerful at this unexpected insight into the peculiar state of affairs in a Northern jail. Jennifer sent back a skirt 'belonging to Patricia', relief all over. I put the skirt on, it fitted. The screws were like small children, delighted with themselves for solving the problem. Well, with all the changing, what about my seeds?

Alas, another dream. My feet had sweated, the seeds stuck to them, and when I had my bath, the seeds came floating on top as in a stagnant meadow pool. Would they notice? They didn't. I carefully picked them up, dried them, and returned them to my shoes. The rest of the seeds were in my black trousers: I had to transfer them surreptitiously to the skirt. A lot of them disappeared during this process. A large onion seed rolled onto the floor and a screw picked it up. I told her it was an onion seed and she carefully put it away in an envelope with my name on. It had crossed my mind that the whole change of clothes could have been a trick. I told them that if this turned out to be so, I wouldn't wear them.

I was led into the central hall from which the wings radiate. On the left, C Wing, for political-status prisoners—only three of them now there. On the right was A Wing; and in the centre, B Wing.

In the main hall were the television monitors and notices. There are male uniformed prison officers there. Before going into B Wing, I had to go to the surgery. More rabbit warrens up narrow staircases until we reached it. The door wouldn't open, the key wouldn't fit. Inside, girlish voices saying, 'It's no use, it's stuck. We'll have to get the tradesman in—wait.' I was roaring with laughter, I suppose out of sheer nerves, so was the screw. We sat on the stairs.

'This is the North of Ireland', I said.

'Well', she said, 'it's good to have a laugh.'

'Stop everything and laugh for a week and you may see sense,' I said, 'you're all mad up here. Have a vision of a new Ireland and dignity.'

'Well,' she said, 'it would be something different . . .'

The door was eventually unlocked, I was brought into the surgery, made a statement about not co-operating with the medical staff, because they are supposed to be healers and were not, and was brought back to B Wing.

As I came in a group of young girls (juvenile prisoners) in shorts and T-shirts came running through, laughing and panting. 'Enjoying the sunshine, girls?' said the screw. 'Yes,' they chorused. They looked like cheer-leaders in a holiday-camp. Then another girl came in, weeping. A screw had her arm around her, saying, 'Ach now, what's the matter with you?—had bad news on your visit?' Motherly, she pressed the girl closer to her.

I had a clean cell with a contemporary-styled dressing table and fitted wardrobes. Dinner was being served. A towel and soap were given to me. I returned these, as Ann-Marie had done: but nothing happened. 'You won't be going to A Wing until you've seen the Governor,' I was told. 'Here's your dinner, it's really nice today.' It was put on my table. The door was open, a young woman was wheeling her pram along the wing. It was all different from before. Then Jennifer came in.

'Do your clothes fit you all right? I've brought some jeans, they'll be better for you when you go into A Wing.'

She had also brought a cup of tea and some biscuits. She sat down on the bed and said wistfully, 'I can't wait to get into A Wing, there's only four of us on remand, my trial won't be coming up until September.'

'How come you're allowed into this area?'

'Oh, everything is changed now,' she said, 'there is no barrier now between the remand prisoners and the crims. Do you want to come and sit outside in the sun?'

The pram was there: young women talking and smoking. After a bit I came back in. The rule-book was given me to read, a large, red, vellum-covered book. I was trying to study it when another prisoner darted in. 'It's all a lot of bull', she said, 'in the end it's the Governor that decides everything.' She darted back to her own cell. I saw her working on an enormous tapestry of the royal family. Who were the republicans and who were the loyalists? I didn't know. Jennifer came back in with cigarettes. Then a screw came in: 'Jennifer, you'd better go.' She didn't move. The screw left.

After a while Jennifer said, 'I'm not supposed to be here really, good-bye.'

She was so young, so fresh-faced, so pretty, like a young American film-star playing the 'girl-next-door'. How was I going to get into A Wing? I didn't eat or drink anything because I was determined not to use the toilet. I would just have to wait and see what happened the following day.

The door opened at 8.30 a.m.

A screw said, 'Are you going to work?'

I said, 'No, I want to go to A Wing.'

'You'll have to see the Governor first,' she said.

He was in the guard-room. I was brought in there. I said that I'd come into prison to be in A Wing.

He said, 'Don't worry, you'll be taken there, we're not hiding anything from you.'

I repeated my usual formula, challenging his role as an unquestioning servant of the British government. When I'd finished, I went back to my cell, pissed in my pot, rang the bell, and said, 'I want to go to A Wing. If I'm not taken, I'm going to throw this piss on the floor.' Like a shot, I was taken out of B Wing. So it was easy after all. On the way through the central hall, I met the screw who was to take me to A Wing.

'Ha,' she said, 'you see the transformation.' She was now wearing a navy-blue jump-suit, white boots, a white mask. 'Don't you

think it's smart?' (I was holding my breath) 'The smell isn't all that
bad.'

A Wing: dark, gloomy, it was like going into hell, the screws all
muffled up, soft feet in their boots, very quiet. I was taken into a
cell. Babs and Briege, whom I had met before, were there. The cell
was dark, reminiscent of a room in some hostel for derelicts, three
iron bedsteads, a bowl full of slop, dark smears on the wall, the
atmosphere very musty. The two of them were lying in their beds,
grey and neglected-looking. I didn't want to stare too much. They
were smiling, however, and very self-contained.

Babs passed me a beautifully thin roll-up. I had arrived: and there
was tobacco. Yes, three roll-ups a day. Babs was a genius and used
to break hers up to make about fifteen very thin ones. The cell door
opened, and Babs went out, returning almost at once with salads. I
couldn't eat; most of the food was thrown into the bowl. It was
over-flowing. 'Excuse me,' Briege said as she disappeared behind
her bed, crouching down. She and Babs exchanged banter whilst
the operation was taking place. God, I'll never be able to do it, I
thought.

The cell door opened again. 'Come this way.' I was taken out and
put into an empty cell. Cream-coloured walls, perforated and
scarred, two beds and a plastic bowl. I sat on the bed, the door
opened again, it was Liz. We sat facing each other, smiling.
'Phew. . . . !

7.   **First Impressions of A Wing**

> It is solely by risking that freedom is obtained
> . . . the individual who has not staked his or her life may,
> no doubt, be recognised as a Person; but he or she has not
> attained the truth of this recognition as an independent
> self-consciousness. Hegel *The Phenomenology of Mind*

16 May 1980: last night I dreamed I was on my bicycle pedalling
along a white mountain road. On the right-hand side the heather

was in bloom; I smelt it and felt happy. I found myself pedalling downhill to where there was a mill-stream. The millwheel was at the bridge and there were two men stooping over it. I pedalled down towards the stream, splashing my legs as I cycled through the sparkling water. I felt the water on my leg and I woke up. I shouldn't have had that dream, the water should not have touched my leg. Another dream: I am out with my mother; we are walking along a London suburban street; it is summer; the gardens are full of flowers—roses, bright green trees along the road, bright green open spaces. I shouldn't be here: I must go back, I have betrayed my comrades. How did I get out, why did I think I could leave for the day and then gaily return to my cell?

Thus the subconscious works. I was free if I wanted to be, I could leave—but why didn't I want to? My perceptions going through the layers of the mind, or as in a Hitchcock film, from room to room, nearer to the moment of understanding. So my visit to Armagh Jail—non-payment of a fine. Won't pay for the privilege of speaking the truth. Easy slogan: but not so easy to arrive at the point of speaking it and meaning it.

I am in jail in 'Northern Ireland' with thirty other young women whom I do not see. I am now in a cell with Liz: we are together. Mairead has not been given permission to advise us.

Once a day we go out into the yard. Mairead goes out an hour after us. The sun is shining. It is a small yard, a prison yard, high walls, old wall crumbling at the crevices, a sprawling rock-flower grows in the crumbling plaster. We don't know anyone, we are eager to make ourselves acceptable.

Liz has cigarettes. She takes a cigarette and offers the packet. 'I was able to bring in a packet.' They politely decline. We lean our backs against the wall, smoking. I have nothing to say. Liz lives in Belfast. 'Do you know the Rock Bar? That's where I drink.' Our hour is up. We are back in our cell. We lie on our beds. I am tired, I fall asleep as soon as I get in. Our cell walls are shining, cream-coloured, clean. We look at the walls and are ashamed.

'I always shit once a day,' Liz says.

What are my shitting habits? Not regular: if I eat I will shit. But I can't shit. What will happen if I don't shit for three months?

What will happen to the piled-up food in my stomach? Does shit always come out?

'Yes' she says, 'it will.'

What about piles? Ads flash through my mind, small bleeding ulcers encircling the anus like fungi.

'I had piles when I was pregnant, it was no bother. You can get a suppository from the surgery.'

I am not going to the surgery. I announced that when I arrived. Doctors; nurses, blue and shiny, with white collars and cuffs, and gleaming trays with little bottles of pills. Nazi Germany. They perpetuate what is going on. 'You have abdicated your responsibilities as healers,' I sloganise when I arrive. I prefer my bowels to petrify. I am tired. I go to sleep.

Some of them eat bread and marge. We look at one another. We will never eat bread and marge. We are not hungry. Well, we certainly won't be getting hungry here, because we are not going to use up any energy. One hour in the yard. If I eat as little as possible maybe my stomach won't have sufficient food to petrify inside. I think of plumbing, cottage plumbing. Shit spilling over blocked drains. My body after all is only the original plumbing-plan for our sanitary civilization. Simply eat as little as possible and there is no problem. But what about our obligation to cover our walls. . .? I am tired, the familiar Morpheus waiting for me. We must shit. I can't.

'Liz, you shit once a day, you've eaten half a bowl of cornflakes, it must come out.'

She squats on newspaper. I close my eyes, plug up my ears, turn on my side, minutes pass: I hear rustling movement. She had gone back to her bed.

'Any luck?'

She shakes her head.

'I'll have to go when you're asleep,' I say. I am embarrassed, in case I fart and smell. How do they do it? Rose had told me she always puked. 'You want to puke?'

'Yes,' Liz said, 'I can't help it, it's just a reaction, it's not you.'

'I know. We haven't gone yet.

'Any decorating done yet?' a voice whispers in the spyhole in a broad North of Ireland accent I can hardly follow. Liz is able to catch it, she smiles.

'Not yet'.

'Don't worry,' the voice says, and goes away. Doors lock and unlock, voices whisper in to us. 'Any decorating done yet?'

Liz sits on the bed shaking.

'I'm sweating,' she says. 'Sweat is pouring off me and I'm shaking. It's the same shaking as when I visit Gerard in the Block. He shakes all the time.'

I am not shaking and I am not sweating; but I am tired. I cannot think: I am numb. My concentration is on my bowels, on my stomach. Move, I think, move. I am passive, like in a hospital waiting for childbirth, waiting for deeper contractions, the birth of my shit.

'I think I'm going to go, Liz—quick, plug your ears, close your eyes, turn your face to the wall.'

I get some tissues, lay them on the floor, squat. I must relax. Contractions are going away. I will piss, where is the pot? I heave myself over. Piss. Must not shit with the piss. Move back on to the tissue. I pull my knickers up, then my jeans. Nothing. Nothing. Days pass: I remain absorbed in my lack of shit. I am not aware of anything, only the task of shitting. After breakfast one morning, Liz shits.

'I've had a shit, I've had a shit, it's small and brown, hard as a nugget.' Carefully wrapped up in a tissue.

She takes it to the wall. I want to puke. My nostrils are closed, I close my eyes. I open. She has covered a small section of the walls—a swirl, a small swirl, Liz has done it. The next voice exclaims: 'I see you've started decorating, Liz!'

I am a failure. I must. I must. That night I produce a little one, a sheep's one. Is that all? What about all the food I ate before coming in, bacon, sausage, ice cream, two slices of fried bread and an egg in the police station, the food I'd eaten in here, is it all contained in this small hard nut? I apply it to the wall, I press hard, it falls off. I pick it up again, pressing it more lightly, as though I was touching a glass for a table-rapping session at a séance; let it take itself over the wall; it moves in thin lines. I am proud. The next time I shit I am going to draw pictures. My drawing is lousy. I will practise. I lie on the bed and look at my shit. It is beautiful. It doesn't smell. We lie on our beds looking at our shit. A voice comes.

This time we ask them: 'How are *you* getting on with *your* decorating?'

'We're covered our cell twice, we are on the third go.'

We go back to bed and sleep.

There is always a sing-song for new arrivals on their first night; we must all have a song ready. We drag our beds up to the outside wall and stand on the railing, pressing our faces to the window—a prison-window with bars outside it, and a board where two of the panes are broken. We yell our song 'The Women's Army is marching'—cheers, stamping. 'Again,' they cry. We strain our voices. We are elated. 'More, more!' they shout. We try to remember snatches of other songs. Liz is very good; she sings the H Block song:

> I'll wear no convict uniform, nor meekly serve my time
> That Britain might brand Ireland's fight eight hundred years of crime.

I sing in unison. Liz has a strong clear voice. She is able to keep in tune. The resonance of our voices in the high cell sounds harmonious. Everyone sings. We hear bright clear young voices like angels—each one sings a solo. 'Four Green Fields'. We are in heaven. It's fantastic, fantastic.

Ann-Marie had told us about this spirit. Prisoners of War. The fighting goes on in here as well as outside. These young women all singing their defiance of Britain's right to rule Ireland. Midnight: it all stops. There is silence. The magic is over. I am happy. 'Good night, Liz'. She is so beautiful, her smile, her white teeth, blonde hair. We are girls back in the dorm, whispering together. But we are also women asserting our right to choose. We are free.

'Good-nights' echo in the wing. The night-guard's feet are heard, up and down, turning the lights off. I pull the grey blanket over me. The guard-dogs bark outside, men's gruff voices calling them. The powerful lamps encircling the jail are switched on. The cameras and TV monitors. We are in the most highly protected of all the jails in the United Kingdom, made especially secure because

of two young women, the Price sisters, who were brought back here
from England after their 76-day hunger strike. We'll be going to
Mass tomorrow and will see the other prisoners for the first time.
'Good night, Liz'; 'Good night, Margaretta.' It was all so easy, it
was all so beautiful.

> If I could, I surely would
> Stand where my militant sisters stood!

We were at last with our sisters.

We were high with relief at being in Armagh. At this stage we
only experienced the commitment of the other women through the
evening entertainments shouted out through the heavy steel cell
doors. We were locked up all day except for one hour: and as only
two at a time were allowed out on the wing, Liz and I had hardly
any contact with the other prisoners. Liz said we should separate
and each try to share a cell with a regular prisoner. But at this stage
it didn't seem possible. Since 7 February 'marriages' had been
made—two women sharing each cell. Indeed it was Mairead's
policy as O.C. that no prisoner should be on her own at the
beginning.

Liz and I adjusted to one another. Although we were both members
of Women Against Imperialism, I had hardly known her, because
my relationship with the group had been so tenuous.

8. A Wing Routine

> Jail is a very dehumanising experience. But especially in
> the situation we were in, when we were being harassed to
> get us off the protest. You lose your femininity com-
> pletely, you become very hard in your attitudes, your
> speech, in every way, because you have to, in order to
> survive in jail. Maureen Gibson, ex-Armagh prisoner

The top floor of the wing is unoccupied. The cell doors are open,
showing empty association rooms, empty toilets and wash basins,

empty showers and baths, empty kitchens, empty laundry. The male screws sometimes sit in one of the association rooms here, watching the TV. The chapel is also on the top floor. The stairs leading up from the bottom of A Wing are boarded up, and a special door is unlocked for us when we go to Mass. We go along the top, beside the horizontal wire-netting stretched across the wing in the mid-seventies when there was a riot in sympathy with the burning of the Kesh. Bedsteads, plates and food, which were thrown over during the riot, are still caught in the meshing. When we go through on our way to Mass, it is like traversing a ghost-town, all shining and empty. The chapel is a room at the end adaptable for use by both Roman Catholics and Church of Ireland: it is also the cinema. The screws change the statues, flowers, etc., for different services. There are benches; the room has a coved ceiling and cream-coloured walls, three doors—one for each wing—there is a retiring room for confessions. All the RC prisoners in the jail (including the men) meet there at Mass.

On our ground floor there are about eighteen cells on each side, two guard-rooms, each with a table and chair, an electric kettle, and a small hotplate for the use of the screws. There is an association room, with chairs laid out, facing towards a table where there should be a television. This room is always open, always expectant. There is one set of toilets with three wash basins and one shower room where the male guards clean themselves after cleaning the cells. There is a long, shining hotplate opposite the door which leads into the yard. There are two blocked-up staircases down from the top floor.

Except in the case of two cells which used to be association rooms, and which contain three girls each, there are two girls in each 11ft by 8ft cell. All the fittings have been removed. Each ordinary cell contains two iron beds, with the iron bed-springs soldered to the frames so that they cannot be detached; two thin foam-rubber mattresses; three grey blankets; two pillows, sometimes made of straw; one plastic po (some of the poes have lids); a large plastic bowl, uncovered, for slops. In some of the cells there are small cupboards with shelves. We have one blue plastic mug each, and a thermos flask. We are given a toothbrush, paste, comb; and have a transparent plastic container which once contained disinfectant but is now used for water.

7.30 a.m. the female and male screws come on the wing, our master-locks are unlocked, the 'spy' is opened and we are counted. There is much laughter. Then the long process of going for breakfast begins. Only one cell is unlocked at a time, which means that only two girls are out on the wing at one time. The screws line the wing as we go down to collect the food. There would be from 16 to 20 female screws. The men are upstairs standing by the entrance. We take it in turns to go up for the breakfast.

First the cell is opened. We push the door back, and empty the thermos flask from last night into the bowl which already contains our overnight urine. We then throw these slops out onto the wing, avoiding the screws who are standing there. If we were to throw it *at* them, they would instantly crowd in and attack the individual prisoner. It has to be thrown high up the wing so that it flows down. Then the bowl is returned empty into the cell. You take the blue mug and thermos flask, hand the mug over at the hotplate where there is an open container of milk. A ladleful is poured into the mug, ¼ pint each. You also hand over the flask which is filled with tea from an urn. The urn has to be filled from an ordinary electric kettle, so the first one out gets very strong tea. They ladle tea leaves for thirty women into the urn, only gradually renewing the hot water from the kettle as the tea is poured out.

Pale blue plastic bowls are laid out, one-third full of cornflakes. Beside them is a wall-safe with marge, sugar, salt. There is also a breadbin. It takes a couple of journeys back to the cell to carry the thermos flask, mug and bowl of cornflakes with spoons. When you are back in the cell the door is locked, the peep-hole is bolted. The food is put on the cupboard and covered with tissues, if there are any. If there is no cupboard, it is put on the floor. We go back to bed. This process takes about an hour and a half.

Outside there is continuous noise of doors being locked and unlocked, slops being thrown out, feet pattering, the wait, then the feet coming back. All through this the jangling of keys, impatient if they think that one of the women is too slow. At about 9.30 there is the noise of locking and unlocking of doors once again as the screw puts an arm in to collect the empty bowls. At 9.50 Mairead the O.C. calls the roll. Every woman answers 'Aye'. She will repeat the name until she hears a reply. We then get up, make our beds, dress.

The next part of the routine changed twice while I was there. When I first came in, there were four batches of eight girls each going for exercise from 10 to 11, 11 to 12, 2 to 3 and 3 to 4 respectively. The process of calling in each batch two at a time became too cumbersome, as it meant that the first batch weren't all in till 12.30. So after ten days it was changed to allow sixteen to exercise in the yard at a time, from 10.15 to 11.15 a.m., and 2 to 3 p.m.

At 12 o'clock dinner was up. The long process of unlocking and locking, slops being thrown out, and prisoners going two at a time to collect the dinner, one pale plastic fork, plastic knife, plastic plate and pudding-bowl. This was also the time for messages between the cells; as soon as the cell was open, one would dart to deliver or to ask someone in another cell to deliver a message to yet another cell when they came out. Occupants would call out for a visit, we'd be scurrying up and down, through the slops—trying not to skid—all amid the clamour of the screws calling us to collect the dinner. Having collected the dinner, we'd put it into the cell, dart out again to deliver more messages, and all the time the screws were calling to get the women back—like a farmyard where the farmer is trying to get two little piglets at a time back into the sty, or a disorderly infants' playgroup. Prisoners call out asking if anyone likes the dinner or wants someone else's. Prisoners at the far end call: 'What's for dinner?' Anxiety mounts behind the locked doors in case a favourite dish runs out before one can get to it.

There is no regular order for unlocking the cells. Doors are chosen at random, so you never know, except by the jangling outside your cell, when your particular door is going to be opened. All this happens very quickly: a neurotic hustle and bustle, until, at about 1.30, we're all locked up again. Then the process begins once more of screws taking away the plates, unlocking and locking doors, getting stuck, wrong keys, wrong cells.

Two o'clock: exercise time. More unlocking and locking of doors. Each time we go out we empty our slops. After each exit, the male crims come on the wing to clean up the slops—six times a day. Between two and four p.m. the post arrives. Unlock doors, lock doors, wrong doors, wrong letters. Four o'clock—tea. Once again, the confusions of a railway station, a hospital emergency ward, a Naples tenement. On Wednesday and Saturday the visitors' bus arrives, with post, tissues, stamps, and religious magazines. More unlocking, signing for parcels. 5.30: doors open again for plates: 7.30, supper. Water containers are filled up at this time. No-one is allowed out of the cells after 7.30, so if supper has not been served by then the screws have to go slopping up and down handing in the supper and filling the water. There are no plates involved at supper. 8.30 p.m., the master-lock on each cell is clicked, no-one on the wing can open them. The master-locks are kept in a central office.

9 p.m. the Rosary in Irish; then calling out for that evening's 'entertainment'. 10 p.m. the entertainment begins. Three nights a week Irish language classes; a lecture; a quiz; bingo: and one free night. At 12 p.m. we say goodnight, there is no more shouting, we whisper in our cells, write our letters, read our magazines. If you want the lights out, you press a buzzer. The solitary guard hears the click and switches the light off from outside. When it gets dark the enormous arc lamps surrounding the prison light up, the guard-dogs come into the yard barking. The male patrol calls his dog, there's a crashing outside, banging the windows and jeering obscene insults at us. Every hour during the twenty-four the telephone rings, for a screw to reassure the office, police army barracks, that there are no riots. At dawn the prison is buzzed for fifteen minutes by a helicopter, it swoops over and over the jail, encircling it. At about 9 p.m. practice alarms go off to coincide with alarms in the army barracks and the RUC station. In the evening the remand prisoners in B Wing shout over to us the news they have heard on their radio.

Every fourth Monday a screw opens your cell door at 8.30 a.m. and says 'Work?' No reply. She goes out. Between 10.30 and 11.00 the Governor comes around for what is known as Adjudication. It is in fact a trial. The Governor, the Assistant Governor, the chief female prison officer of the jail, the chief female prison officer of the wing, and a P.O. as witness, all arrive and the witness-screw testifies, 'At

8.30 a.m. on 18 May I entered M. D'Arcy's cell and asked if she was available for work. She replied that she was not available.' Governor: 'Do you plead guilty or not guilty? For refusing to work you lose remission for four weeks. Under section something-or-other you lose the following privileges: filmshows three visits books television radio parcels' and so on. It's all rattled off at such a speed it's impossible to hear. No-one has time to answer. As soon as the posse arrives, one of us is asked to leave the cell so the adjudication takes place with only one prisoner present at a time. The woman outside is supposed to be standing meekly outside and then vice-versa. The prisoner being adjudicated usually lies on her bed reading or deliberately turns her face to the wall. There is no suggestion that the Governor or the prison officers are seriously concerned to get the women off the protest, or even to wait for the answers. It is a ritual, and as soon as it's done they move on to the next cell.

On Saturdays the locum doctor comes in, says 'How're ye, ladies?' and walks out again. At irregular intervals, everyone is asked to go individually to the surgery, to be weighed and have her blood-pressure taken, usually after a heavy meal; there is no warning and therefore the women are not necessarily weighed in the same quantity of clothes as they were the previous time. Surgery: the nurse comes round with a tray of pills, stands at each cell and gives them out to those who want them. Once a month on a fixed day, whether we are menstruating or not just then, she gives out either sanitary towels or tampax (you can't have both). The quantity is the same for each prisoner, no matter how heavy or light her period. Prison visitors come once a fortnight but do not visit the cells. Father Murray comes twice a week to visit each cell in rotation. There is Confession once a week, on Saturday: Mass on Sunday at nine: and on Saturday mornings the Legion of Mary are allowed in, 'on a visit of mercy', to say the Rosary Novena in the chapel with any prisoner who wishes to attend. The St Vincent de Paul Society is permitted to send in a couple of copies of *The Irish News* at irregular intervals: and also some Sunday newspapers, such as the *Sunday News* or the *Sunday Press*. There is an official Prison Welfare Officer whose job is to liaise between the prisoners and their families. Fr Murray has provided Bibles for the prisoners and their relatives send in religious magazines. This is all the reading matter permitted for those on the protest.

9. A Wing Self-Sufficiency

> Free people cannot be kept in jail, for their spirits are free, and jail for political prisoners is always a duel. We were not prisoners of war, no prisoner had been conceded political rights, and the duel went on. . . . jailors and wardens have to peep and pry, to be ever on the alert, to glue their eyes to keyholes, to listen at cell doors, and to deal with what to them is an unknown quantity—the spirit of freedom. There was a tendency to think in terms of one's immediate surroundings: food; warders, their sayings and doings, their tricks of speech and idio-syncrasies. Sometimes one would discover that a greater part of one's thoughts was taken up with the trivial happenings of the day, the doings of the little automatons that help to keep one captive. That is the danger point.
> Ernie O'Malley, *The Singing Flame*. August—October 1923.

Our own organisation inside A Wing (that is, the 'A Wing Company IRA'). There is the prisoner O.C., normally appointed from the outside by the IRA. She in turn appoints her own staff from among her fellow prisoners: Entertainment Officer, Welfare Officer, Quartermaster, and her Second-in-Command.

No-one has any direct contact with any of the prison staff, including the Governor, except through the O.C., who requests interviews with the Governor on the women's behalf. If you are ill, you ask the O.C. to ask the surgery to call. She will also call the official Prison Welfare Officer if there is a family problem. Our own Welfare Officer organises the visits, fills in the cards, and so on. If there are any problems about letters, she deals with the censor. The Entertainment Officer organises the nightly entertainments to keep up the morale. The Quartermaster is responsible for getting the Company's tobacco smuggled in and for doling out the ration of three thin roll-ups per day.

The overall running of the wing is done by the O.C., who has a weekly consultation with the Governor. She also allocates cells, and permits changes of cells. She is consulted on any new developments between the Northern Ireland Office and the Governor. She will then call a meeting in the yard, and decisions are taken by majority vote, the O.C. acting as chairperson. Because the Company was divided for exercise into two groups of sixteen, she appointed her Second-in-Command to chair the other group. Once a week she is allowed by the Governor to spend an evening discussing Company business with her Second-in-Command in the latter's cell.

The O.C. decides whether non-IRA political prisoners are to be accepted as 'honorary members' of the Company. Liz and I were accepted; we attended meetings for prison business but not for Company affairs. The O.C. also organises groups of six prisoners to prepare propaganda documents to be smuggled out; and she is responsible for contacts between the Company and republicans outside. She has no privileges at all inside the wing—she does not, for instance, get first look at the papers, nor is she let out of her cell in advance of the others to get her meals. Apart from her responsibility as O.C., there is no distinction between her and the other volunteers.

The internal discipline of the Company within the jail. There is no communication between us and the screws: if you have any dealings with them, for instance when collecting the food, you state your requirement, you do not request, you do not say 'please' or 'thank you.' This is one of the hardest things to do, because the words are so automatic. One never becomes aggressive to the screws, but always tries to maintain one's consciousness that one is a prisoner of war and that they are servants of British Imperialism. We do not stoop to their level. I suppose in many respects the code of conduct would be similar to that of a novitiate house: consideration at all times for your cellmate: preservation of mutual solidarity, never allowing quarrels to become public outside the cell, never letting the screws see disunity. Never allow British propaganda that we are sub-human animals to be confirmed by our behaviour. An aloof and dignified demeanour. Do not let the screw hear you swearing. The strategy of the screws seems to be to try and break down this dignity by petty harassment, and to destroy the unity of the prisoners.

Examples of what we took to be harassment: in-coming mail would 'get lost'; prisoners' letters would be read and the contents laughed at; photos sent in would 'get lost'; parcels of tissues and religious magazines would be delivered broken; only a portion of the food supplied would be served, and the rest thrown out; food would be distributed unequally; food would be apparently deliberately allowed to go cold, particularly fried dishes; certain prisoners seemed to be picked on for rough searches, in an attempt to provoke aggro; the screws would curse and swear under their breath about us; slops would be shoved back under cell doors when the wing was being cleaned; prisoners' buzzers would go unanswered and the writing paper we were entitled to would not be supplied.

This sense of harassment alternated with pathetic attempts to woo us.

Our strategy was to break down the screws' morale by ignoring all their moods, in the spirit of neo-Gandhian nonviolent resistance. And this despite the fact that none of the prisoners had ever been involved in a nonviolent movement outside the jail; indeed no such thing exists in the North of Ireland. The ordinary life of the ghetto is anything but nonviolent. The struggle to survive inside a large family made for very strong and individual women well accustomed to fighting back. If they ever allowed another member of the family to take advantage of them, they'd be finished. On the other hand the ghetto culture did make for strong unity against any outside attack.

10.   Jailors and the Jailed

My experience on the protest has made me even more cynical towards the whole system of so-called British 'justice' and 'fair play'. Eileen McConville—ex-Armagh prisoner

The Northern Ireland Office has emphatically repeated that there are no male screws on the wing, only 'tradesmen'. But of course the tradesmen are screws, trained in the prison service as craft-workers who can be used to exercise force where necessary. The prime function of these men on A Wing is to clean the cells: but some of the girls recognised some of them as having been involved in the events of 7 February. There is also no doubt that they were there to give the female screws physical support if needed at any time. They wear bright green dungaree outfits, green boots, and large helmets with visors pulled down over their faces. They carry chemical packs on their backs and use these with other machinery to remove excreta from the walls. They occupy the TV room upstairs; and they hang around the wing and in and around the guard-room.

They were not supposed to be on the wing when we came out of our cells: but we would see them loitering there nonetheless. They would also harass us by peering into our spies. The ones I saw were tall and blond, very virile, looking like characters out of *Star Wars*. There seemed to be about six or eight of them.

Male prisoners from the Crumlin Road Jail, Belfast (all loyalists, I was told) lived in a special section of Armagh Jail. They clean the wing (but not the cells) five or six times a day. This was work normally done by the non-political female prisoners; but since the no-wash protest began it was given to men. The Armagh male crims refused to do it and the ones brought in from the Crum got special privileges—extra remission, extra money, and better treatment almost as if they were screws. We could hear them quarrelling and cursing among themselves as they worked, and they took revenge on us by deliberately shoving slops and disinfectant back under our doors. When cleaning the outside walls they would often point the hoses into the windows and soak the cells with water.

The female prison officers were one of the biggest surprises—not only for me but for the women from the ghettos. In their twenties, well-made, attractive. They were certainly a different breed from the middle-aged and elderly ones. They were nearly all married, some of them appeared to have active love-lives to the detriment of their home life. There was a fast turnover, new faces appearing all the time. Some of them had been through the entire range of security forces, attracted by the ever-ready handouts from the British government to entice recruitment. I suppose they would have joined the Army for three years, left with a handout, then the RUC, more handouts, and now they had become prison officers. This was the most highly-paid section of the security forces.

Stretched out on my bed I would peruse *The Irish News*, from front to back, and front again, to be faced with half-page ads recruiting prison officers, £8,000 to start with, allowances for houses, overtime, daily allowances. One of the girls had heard a screw saying to another: 'I got £280 into my hand this week.' They must be bringing home annually up to £20,000. No wonder they look like superhumans.

There was a cell next door to the guard-room, where they sat and drank coffee, and chatted from morning till night, chasing each other in and out like kids. Their conversation could be overheard— their assignations with male screws for the evening. They could sleep in the jail if they wanted to. They had their own flats. One of them was notorious: christened by the screws 'the marriage-breaker', she was divorced with one child. An overheard conversation one Christmas went down in jail memory as 'the total collapse of womanhood'. She always worked overtime. The child was looked after by her mother. On Christmas Eve she was heard asking the other screws what she should buy her seven-year-old child for Christmas.

Their main conversation was about the amount of booze they had drunk the night before, or else what kind of boxes of chocolate their husbands had given them if they were 'nice' to them. 'He brought me a big box of coffee-creams, I told him that was no good, as I didn't like them. He then went out and bought a different box, I let him have a quick one.' Giggle giggle, high-pitched squeals, 'She fancied him but she didn't get a look in with him because of her. There she was lying in bed with him trying to get his thing up when your woman walks in wearing nothing but black lace knickers etc . . .' It seemed to be a non-stop soft-porn show. Then you could hear the deep bass tones of laughter from the male screws.

I once peeped out of my spy to see them piggy-backing up and down the wing, collapsed with laughter, the male screws running after them. The more asexual we became with our loose-fitting jeans and streaks of dirt running down our faces, the more feminine they became, with their elaborate coiffures, their waists nipped in tightly, great whiffs of perfume choking our nostrils every time we left the cells. Constantly standing around smoking king-sized filter cigarettes, they would blow the smoke into our faces as we passed by. Sometimes they would deliberately stand outside our cell doors, speculating about what they would have for dinner: strawberries and ice cream, a trifle, or maybe just a cream bun.

We never rose to their bait: the more trivial they became, the more we despised them. At times they desperately looked towards us for a smile or some sort of recognition that they were there, but they never got it. One day Shirley was passing on the wing and saw a gold watch lying there. One of the screws must have dropped it. She wondered if she shouldn't walk on it, but she thought, 'Why should I become like them?' With dignity she said, 'You've dropped your watch.' The screw had to rummage in the running slops to retrieve it.

Were the Screws frightened of us? Did some of them think that by smiling at us they would escape assassination? The IRA policy was 'execution of screws'. How much did they think of the reality of their death? An 'execution' of female screws took place in the early summer of 1979, (two months after our first demo on 8 March), when the INLA shot four screws in the road in front of the jail, killing one. Was the women's movement in any way responsible, by highlighting the women prisoners of war? The dead one's sister worked on A Wing—a subdued washed-out blonde. After the shooting the prisoners had been locked up for three days, until the funeral had taken place. Several screws resigned their jobs afterwards. There had been a lot of tension, but I didn't get a sense that the prisoners (or the screws) felt that there was any direct relationship between them and the snipers.

I witnessed something of the fear caused to the screws by the prisoners on 9 August, the anniversary of Internment, when we banged our doors and windows and pipes with our plastic mugs and roared out rebel songs from four to five in the morning (the time when the houses were raided). This is an annual ritual in Northern jails. The following morning only six of us were fresh enough to go out during the exercise period; and we sang more rebel songs outside:

> What'll we do with the prison screws?
> Shoot shoot shoot the bastards!

As I was going in, I saw them laughing hysterically and they certainly looked frightened. Who was the jailor and who the jailed in this bizarre prison? They had to have strict security to protect them going in and out of the jail. They couldn't sit in any pub or go where they chose outside. What did they think of us?

Did we have power of life and death over them? I found myself quite indifferent to their fate. I was never able to see them as individuals. It made me realise how stupid I had been to think that I could have broken through to them. They were equally unable to see us as individuals. For as long as they wore the uniform we would be at war with them. There would have been no personal sorrow if they had all been wiped out. They had all taken part in the assault of 7 February. The ones that were thought to be the most kind, had turned out to be the most ferocious. It is not pleasant to find oneself turning into a stone and becoming indifferent.

The policy in A Wing was not to abuse screws, just not to acknowledge their presence. The screws didn't like this, it rattled them. Some of them, particularly the more athletic ones, longed for a scrap. They tried to pick on some of the women; in particular Linn from Derry, I don't know why. One dinner-time we heard Linn's voice raised. I wasn't in long enough to realise that this was something new. Afterward, in the yard, Linn came out ashen-faced and trembling. She told us that one of the screws had positioned herself at the hotplate, and was dancing on her toes, one hand pounding into the other, and screaming, 'Come on take me on, or are you yellow?' The other screws were lined up, nervously saying, 'Cool it,' to her, but she went on screaming and laughing. Linn and Sadie had come out of their cell to collect their dinner. When they saw what was happening, they returned to the cell, but the screw kept on shouting 'Come on!' Linn just stood there and turned around to her, saying quietly, 'I don't feel like taking on seven of you.' And she walked very slowly to collect her dinner. The screws were all gathered at one end together: it was very frightening because if the fighting screw had attacked Linn then all the other screws would have joined in to show solidarity.

We were always nervous coming out for meals, because this was the time we were alone. We could not show fear. That would set the screws off. The whole atmosphere of the meal-times was tense. We were constantly standing around in our slops, rivers of urine, sanitary towels, and left-over food floating down the wing. Then there was the ever-thick crowd of flies over the hotplate. In the beginning I had to nerve myself to walk through this putrid stench; sometimes my slop would splash up and splash against my bare leg. I could never look down or I would have vomited. In the beginning of my stay there was a dead grey mouse caught in the skirting board outside the cell. The drying and cleaning machine never caught up all the debris, even though the wing was cleaned five times a day.

11.   Wise Virgins

Mairead and others used to ride their bicycles to school and, coming over Blacks Road, youths would try to pull them off their bicycles. So then Mairead couldn't go on her bicycle but had to go on the bus. Well, the bus went over Blacks Road but that had to be stopped because the bus was attacked. So then the bus had to go far away out by Lisburn to get to Rathmore—which is not far away, you could nearly see it from our upstairs windows—and had to do about a four-mile detour to get to the school. I would think that's contributed to her being where she is now. Mrs Farrell, mother of Armagh prisoner Mairead Farrell

On August 15th in 1969 I can remember the screaming from Bombay Street when the Loyalists led by the brave Specials came up Cupar Street from the Shankhill. I remembered Gerard McAuley being shot while defending the area. Maureen Gibson: ex-Armagh prisoner

My initial contact with the other prisoners made me feel like one of the villains of a Brechtian play, self-centred, individualist, used to an explosive and intensely vigorous public life. In my own house with four sons and a husband, I had had to resist their pressure to turn me into nothing but a nanny-housekeeper. So I was not used to this equal and whole unit. I had to accustom myself to the idea that in Armagh we were truly a community; and that at all times I had to think of and relate my actions to the community. At the same time I had to make sure the community values were genuine and not just a neo-Victorian Catholic reflex.

I was not going to do any heroics inside the jail, nor develop non-violent tactics beyond the point of going inside. I was very aware of the need to respect the delicate balance that already obtained in Armagh. It would have been easy to go in with tremendous energy, crash around, and then leave. But what about the young women serving 20 years and more? The more I understood of their protest, the more I marvelled at their skilful pacing of it. Too much would have meant that too many might have collapsed with the strain; too little, and they could have become demoralised.

Mairead had developed into a highly sophisticated negotiator. She had been there for four years, and in that time to have built and maintained unity among this small group of women was really remarkable. Each of them would come in, alone: having been broken down in Castlereagh and made to sign forced confessions which might implicate innocent people.

They would be on remand for years sometimes before they came to trial. Then they suffered the pressures from the lawyers to acept plea-bargaining arrangements. Then the sentences—it was immaterial whether they were in fact guilty or innocent of the crime said to have been committed—once they got that far along the conveyor belt the sentences were nearly always enormous in the hope that they would accept criminalisation and thus receive 50 per cent remission. So how, after all this, could they show so much unity and so much moral strength? The criminalisation policy had after all been designed exactly to prevent this happening.

But once the Republican Movement had decided to reject criminalisation, and once each prisoner on the protest had experienced for herself the ferocity with which the protest had been countered, the very act of standing firm created its own unity and indeed formed out of these inexperienced and politically-half-educated young women a totally new kind of republican—whose ominous evolution the authorities have even yet not fully understood.

They had another obstacle to contend with—institutionalisation. Tim Pat Coogan says in his book, *On the Blanket*, that after eight years any prisoner becomes institutionalised and cannot be readapted into society. If the POWs in the North of Ireland were never to get the remission of sentence they would normally be entitled to, they would have to serve sentences of up to twenty years. They know very well that without the protest they would come out finished. Keeping the no-wash protest going was a life-or-death struggle, a far larger preoccupation than the business of the excreta and filth.

I was only three months in Armagh and in that time I wanted to understand my fellow-prisoners and their relationship to the jail they were in and the government that kept them there. To discover all this was like passing through maze within maze—each one appearing in front of me just as I thought I had successfully threaded the last one. I was not only an observer, I was also a participant and I had to retain my own individuality as a civilian.

Mairead's task was infinitely more intricate—to ride the ever-changing currents and winds affecting life in jail from society outside. Disturbances deriving from the relationships of the Northern Ireland Office with Westminster; pressures via the Catholic Church; via the Unionists; back again to pressures brought against the Catholic Church; from the Vatican via Britain, from America and the elections via Britain; against America via NATO via Britain; against the Northern Ireland Office via the screws; against the Provos via the public and so upon us, inside. The repercussions flowed through the jail from the constant visitors, the press, the British Information Service, the Prison Visitors, security. And how did we know the importance of each new official visitor? By the artistry of Griff, the cook, as revealed in how he prepared and served up our dinner each day.

Add to this the impact of our own visitors, the radio, the newspapers and our letters. Our emotions continually flickered up and down as we sat for 23 hours each day inside our cells. In A Wing prisoners do not feel sorry for themselves: no-one cries, so what outlet is there for emotions, how can we develop and keep flowing the sap that nourishes our humanity?

By passing on each other's personal problems, the girls sympathise with one another and so on, like a chain, thus all problems and sadnesses become collective. One woman, for instance, three months pregnant when she was arrested and refused bail. She grew to 16 stone inside. She was convicted while she was still pregnant and everyone in the jail saw the whole development of her pregnancy. A cell was prepared as a nursery. She had her baby which was brought back to her for only six weeks and then was sent out for her sister to foster. On the day she gave the baby over to her sister, she turned round and said, 'Get rid of all this.' When she came back from the visiting room, all traces of the nursery had vanished. From then on she was alone. Once a month she sees the baby, who is now three. After these visits she passes round the photographs. She is calm, no crying, no talking about her feelings; but the facts are passed on, we whisper about it in our cells, we suffer for her alone in our cells, we salute her courage in remaining on the no-wash protest—for had she come off it, she would gain the remission that would enable her to be at home with her baby *eight years* sooner.

The love and comfort we feel for this young mother, yet can never express to her face, becomes a circle of love enfolding us all. When one suffers, we all suffer, but we never discuss it all together. We never are all together.

After 7 February, only two women at a time were allowed out in the yard, followed by the male screws. Then four, then eight, then sixteen. The male screws are no longer present but we are watched all the time by the female screws and by the television. The screws have their walkie-talkies, and talk into them constantly, as though the whole British and NATO alliance has encircled us and is watching us. We cannot allow them to see our weaknesses, so in the yard we sit, or walk, or jog. The conversation is slack, mainly about the visitors; no huddles of women getting together, no embraces to share grief; as a group we are alone, and individually each one is alone within the group. You cannot become too dependent upon someone else, because at any time she may collapse under the pressures of the no-wash protest, and if that happens, you collapse too. So we remain alone and straight, but together. Hence the watchfulness, the re-examinations, the remembrances of why we are there gnawing into us, never forgotten. We are the seven wise virgins who must always watch and wait.

12.   Getting To Know Them

Mairead Nugent, who was born in Belfast on June 28th 1959, is the eldest of five children and has three brothers and one sister. The family lived in the Iveagh area, off the Falls Road, before moving to Andersonstown in 1965. Mairead was ten years of age when the British army came on to the streets in August 1969, and two years later she became drawn into the struggle as a result of the street protests over internment. She attended all the marches, along with her mother, and witnesses many friends being arrested and being put in jail . . .

Mary Doyle, who was born in Belfast on January 28th 1956, is the eldest of three children, and has two brothers. She was brought up in Greencastle, North Belfast. Mary was attracted to republicanism from an early age, when she wanted to join the Republican Movement, but was turned down on several occasions because of her age. She was first arrested in March 1974 and charged with causing an explosion on the M2 motorway. She was sentenced to five years imprisonment. While Mary was in Armagh jail, her mother was killed in a loyalist bomb attack on Conways Bar, on the Shore Road on March 13th 1975.

Prisoners' biographies, quoted from *Republican News*.

The routine of the day in the cell was simple. Apart from the 60 minutes of exercise daily, the hours of compelled enclosure had a rhythm of their own. The day began quietly, with very little communication either in the cells or between the cells until after four p.m. Letters from Belfast on the visitors' bus, on Wednesdays and Saturdays, brought excitement. The news was exchanged, and then, as we entered into the evening we would talk with our cell-mates next door and to each other. A lot of the time was spent in singing pop songs. Eilis and Ann-Marie would sing together all day and all evening, as did Rosie and Mairead. It was like a humming aviary, joined by the pigeons sitting on the ledge outside. The male screws and crims would also hum and whistle. New songs would be sent in and exchanged. If there was a favourite song being sung on the radio in the workshop, some of the girls in the yard would crowd up against the wall listening. Sentimental love songs, (such as Rod Stewart's) would soothe, and make an escape route to a world of romance and tenderness.

Getting to know my fellow-prisoners on the no-wash protest was a very slow process. We had only the one hour a day together, and I felt like a new girl at school coming in when term is half-way over. Emerging in ones and twos out of the semi-darkness into the bright light of the yard, we would blink and stumble like animals released from cages. The important task was to stretch our legs. We did not at once leap and run but experienced a slow awakening of the body's senses. The girls had a regular routine of partners with whom they would walk around and exchange views or letters. I felt I had to have the discipline of some sort of task, so I used to jog—anything that would engage my body. In the beginning it was for one minute, it grew to fifteen, then twenty-five, up and down the yard. It took about 25 seconds to go from one end to the other. The freedom, just being alone for a moment, was important, to run against the wind and rain was an escape: but it meant that I would never talk to anyone. Then I plucked up courage and attached myself to two who were very fast walkers. Round and round we would go.

Just walking round and round was one of the most difficult things to do. I could not get my mind to roam freely. I was always conscious of the monotony. I needed an unbroken conversation to throw me into another world. Sometimes it would happen. They would bring out a stream of consciousness, back, back in time to childhood memories of the sixties (anywhere else but the North of Ireland, one would take it for the thirties): queuing up on Tuesday mornings at a certain bakery that used to sell its produce at half-price;—the mothers would make the children miss school that day and arm them with a pillow case to queue for five shillings' worth of goods—bread, cakes, buns. Off they would go carrying the pillow cases on their backs. New Year's Eve, when it was the custom for a piece of coal, a new shilling, and a horse, to enter each house. An old man with a horse would make the rounds of the narrow streets in one area of Belfast and at least try to get the horse's head through the doors. The doors were too narrow. Then there were the street-parties, when the mothers and fathers would dance the reels and sets. Dressing up for St Patrick's Day, a green dress and bows, to show they had their colours as well as the 'orangies'.

The stories would well up: the excitement during the 'Ulster Workers' strike, when they camped outside with all the neighbours because the electricity was cut off, sitting around the fire, throwing in potatoes to be baked and someone would come along with a guitar and strum rebel songs. Great long discussions of what you could buy for a shilling, lists of every sort of sweet food—they would repeat how much they loved their mothers and how, when they got out, they would make it up to them for all the exhausting visits they had had to make. They felt that their parents and families had suffered more than they had. As one put it, 'We know what we are enduring, they can only imagine it.' For some of them with elderly parents, there was the fear that the mother or father would be dead before they were out.

They never spoke about unpleasant memories. The terrors and harassments only came out in each separate cell in the dark at night, when they could be whispered while they were lying in bed. I asked one day, how many of them had been in trade unions? They turned round with blank faces. It was as if another world had been ushered in. The problem was, that if a direct question was asked, one's mind went blank, one could not remember. Even when you were writing letters, if you left off and came back in an hour to finish, you could not remember what you had written an hour ago. The same with visits: the tension of knowing that was only for half an hour, once a month, seemed to blank out the mind. We were so wrapped up in the present that, when prisoners left, the gap was filled very quickly. When Liz left, it was as if she had never been there. It was the same when I was to leave. Like very old people, they could only remember what happened years ago, not what happened last week.

Sometimes they would talk about the hilarious times in B Wing at Christmas, when they made illicit liquor with oddments of fruit saved from their dinners and a bit of yeast smuggled in to make the brew. It could have happened only once or twice, but the way they talked about it, it seemed to have been a never-ending process. They would tell about the difficulty of hiding it from the screws (they used to leave it on the Wing, with clothes over it) who would come into the cell, searching frantically but not finding it. Sometimes they did find it and that was the end. But there were no regrets that it had been discovered—memory had transformed it all into a delight. One Christmas the brew was really strong, none of them realised how strong—they were all scoffing it back until they discovered they were all laughing one minute and crying the next.

Sinead worked in an undertakers' firm. They made everything—the laying-out clothes: black suits and white shirts for the prods; blue, black and cream habits for the catholics. Wreaths, coffins. At the age of sixteen she had overall control of the books. She trained a young lad from the wreathmaking department. She was so efficient that when they decided to expand and move outside Belfast they were going to promote her; but she wouldn't leave Belfast. By accepting any job you might end up having to work in a loyalist area, or travel through a loyalist area.

I once asked what was the earliest memory of an awareness of the unionists. One said it was her father putting up a tricolour in the garden for the 1916 commemorations. (It is forbidden in the North of Ireland to fly the tricolour publicly.) Her father was so bigoted and hated the orangies so much, that on the Twelfth of July he used to drive out of Belfast for the day with the family, and if he saw any orangies on the road he would try and run them over. Another's first memory was of an RUC man's daughter being refused service in the local sweet-shop. They were aware that their parents were much more bigoted than they were.

It was strange to hear snatches of stories from the days of '69. The fear of the orangies coming; the crossing and recrossing of the communities as, after the sectarian attacks, the families would have to up sticks and move to other areas. Over and over again I got the impression that the orangies were more frightened of them, although occasionally one would touch a nerve. I shared a cell for a short time with a young girl facing ten years. She attacked me because I made a humorous remark about a wedding photo in the paper (I had said the bridegroom seemed so gentle and smiling, not like a caricature of a hate-ridden presbyterian): and at this time preparations were going on for the Twelfth of July; we could hear the loyalist drums practising outside. She said that if the Brits left, the orangies would come into the jails and slaughter all the republicans. Was it true? Is the North of Ireland a volcano? Coming from the safety of the 26 Counties, I could only have glimpses of the orange paranoia towards the catholics.

Some of the young women in the prison had worked in the new multi-national industries, such as Grundigs, where there were protestant workers alongside catholics. This made great difficulties for the shop-stewards. There were incidents, as when William Whitelaw paid a visit and the union jack was put up over an arch which the catholics had to pass under. They refused and there was a one-day strike. The protestants would never join in any action for better pay: they were so stupid, one girl said, they couldn't see the ends of their own noses. One of the girls worked for an Indian boss. She could never get up in the morning, so he used to call for her in his car, hooting the horn and waiting till she was dressed. He used to slip her extra pound notes in her wage packet. The girls were not conscious of unions. After blanking out at my question about this, some of them said, yes, they were in a union. But they did not know which one. It seems that jobs were there for them to pick and choose at will, although some of them would have had no more than a year working before they were grabbed by the security forces.

Marie enjoyed factory work, leaving frequently to change to another factory. The last one was a car-assembly plant, where she

fitted the electric wires for the doors. Even when they were unemployed they didn't seem to take it as a serious problem. Shirley had
worked in an old people's home; and then took a job at Wimpey's in
the middle of Belfast. Dolores had worked in Gallagher's cigarette
factory, which she enjoyed. The money was good. Their view of
the Northern industrial scene bore little resemblance to the
landscape of deprivation and discrimination I had read of in books
and pamphlets. Yet the cracks sometimes showed. One girl had left
her parents' home and roomed with a young married woman who
had just had her first baby. Her husband was inside. The baby was
sick and needed expensive drugs: and they had to burn paper to
keep warm. (Some of the girls of course had been consistently
unemployed; and a few came from a rural background.)

I wondered about the girls' mothers. The mothers would have
been working hard, scraping and saving. Did the mothers ever go
out at night? 'Yes,' they would chorus, 'Me mam has her bingo or
the clubs,' but other images would slip in of fathers having been
interned in the 40s and 50s. 'Dad never speaks, he is very quiet, he
never goes out, he's the one who writes the letters to me, me mam
never does.' (Some of them had no mothers, and some had no
fathers.)

Sometimes they had spectacular fantasy-memories; knives being
thrown at sisters for pinching each other's clothes and pinching
boyfriends. One of them had twin sisters in love with the same
boyfriend. Letters would come in telling us of the saga. How 'me
mam had to separate them with her umbrella and it broke.' Of
younger brothers running wild in the streets and neighbours complaining. One of them remembered as a child having her mouth
washed out with soap because she swore and still sitting there
mouthing the forbidden word, spewing out soap bubbles. Clothes,
they adored clothes, all their wages were spent on new clothes. One
of them would come back from running a message for her boss with
a downcast face: 'What have you seen that you want?' he would say.
'Here's a couple of quid, go out and buy the dress you saw.'

They conveyed a richness of feeling and a sense of the vitality of
hundreds and hundreds of young people in the ghetto struggling to
maintain their identity amid the seething of a huge heap of living,
competing bodies. But it was like life in the nineteenth century:

the paternalism of the bosses; the wee girls who could twist any
elder around their fingers. But now they were really up against
some elders who would not be twisted round their fingers and they
could not understand.

Paternalism was now the way the Governor would decide if they
could write to a fiancé in the Block: 'I haven't seen the proof for this
engagement. What age were you when you got engaged? Seventeen?
That's far too young and he's in for fifteen years and you're in for
twelve. You have no prospects of ever getting married, it's a waste of
time to write.' More work for Mairead. Fiancées are allowed to write,
but the proof had got to be obtained: a letter from a parish priest; and
so it goes on. The young men in the Block similarly claimed that
letters from their girlfriends in Armagh were never delivered. One of
them hadn't received a letter for eleven months; long faces in the
yard. Then, through the complicated maze of communication,
through the visits between Armagh and the Kesh, some messages of
love and hope did get through safely. Sometimes the love affairs
would end abruptly. When this happened, the girls did not regard
themselves as grass-widows, and were very independent about their
feelings. But marriage-vows were something that must never be
broken. One day in the yard they were asking me what I would have
done if I had been sentenced to twelve years. I said that I would not
want John to visit me: I had rather he forgot me and married someone
else: but we could still communicate by letter as friends. One of them
turned on me: 'If he made a promise he's got to keep it, a promise is a
promise!' There was no compromise. Loyalty was the strongest
emotion; a blindness, a pig-headedness used to come through, a
savagery of moral judgement. We had a discussion about a popular
romance, *The Passion After Midnight*, which we had all read on
remand. A young French working girl had been betrayed by her lover
and set out to destroy him. In turn she was destroyed by the
manipulation of a court-case. If she were to plead guilty to a murder,
her life would be saved: but she was tricked and executed. They could
not relate their own unjust court experience to the heroine's: she was
morally wicked and deserved to be punished.

Eilis's area, the Bone, had been pulled down. Her family were in a
new housing estate which she had never seen. Belfast was slowly

changing; the cinema in Broadway was pulled down; even the memories would be out of date. Marriages were broken, children were born—and where were they? But they couldn't think about it for too long, they must live on hope; click, click, the feet would go round. Surely October would bring the concessions. If not October, March. It is not so long to wait.

Christmas dinner to think of, but there would be no Christmas dinner this year, click, click, don't think of that, think of last year.

'Griff really did us proud. We put the tables together in the association room for a Christmas party. He gave us fruit juice, turkey, ham, brussels sprouts. The menu was published in *The Irish News*,' though they were cheated again—all the courses were not given as published. 'But it was good, we ate so much, but still we were cheated.'

A salad for tea, with pickles—Griff was a good cook when he wanted to be. One Easter he came up and when he saw the pork lying cold on the hotplate, he was furious with the screws.

'I have worked hard to prepare a good dinner and you are ruining it, why have you not turned on the hotplate? The food is cold, you are disgusting.'

The female screws looked blank. He took away the food and returned it hot, serving it himself. Christmas, Easter and Hallowe'en: but not any more. One Easter there was cream with the jelly. Griff says the Northern Ireland Office has cut down the money for food. 'If you want chips more than once a week, ask the Northern Ireland Office for money, so I can buy potatoes.'

The women love chips, they dream of chips. Every day in the yard, they call over the wall to the men's yard (the male crims help to prepare the food): 'What's for dinner, is it chips?' Of course, when the chips are served, they are cold, grimy, blackened, they are an illusion, a dream, a hope. The dream and the reality do not come together, so one cannot finish them and they are thrown out in the slops. Pale sodden chips lying there as we walk to the hotplate to get our tea.

'The filth. When you get out, tell them.'

'What is the most important thing you want me to tell them?'

'Tell them everything.'

'But what in particular?'

'You know, you can see for yourself, look at us.'

They are putting too much responsibility on me. Can I cope? Have I worked it out yet? Is there one particular item? I am surviving, they are surviving: but I am only surviving because in a short time I will be free. But will I be free? They are staring at me, we are together till they are free. What is the most important thing? Freedom. Even if they ever get their four demands, they will still be in jail.

Mary Doyle, who was in before, and had had political prisoner status, said: 'They don't know what it's like. It doesn't really change anything, you're still a prisoner. I attended classes, typing, English; but I didn't have the concentration. This time I will.'

The classes they will do. Sinead will do O Level English. 'I never appreciated English when I was at school, the teacher thought I was stupid, but I love reading now.'

Eilis—'I used to be bigoted before I came in, I didn't understand about the orangies, but I do now. I want to study about children.'

When they think of political status, they hope again, their eyes light up. In here they have had time to think about what kind of a new Ireland they want. Never, never, will it be like the old Orange State.

'Freedom of speech, we will discuss everything, everyone's point of view will be listened to.'

We are called back to the filth, the cells covered with flies, little happy flies, stubborn flies, flies that, when you think you've got them, fly out of the windows: dead flies, dried blood of fat flies, smearing shit on the walls, bluebottles that buzz, wasps, earwigs, a mass of menacing nature trying to take over.

Shirley said, 'As sure as I stand here, a mass of flies began encircling my head and they pissed on my Bible, little clear drops of piss, the buggers, they did it deliberately. Then one big one came towards me, its eyes fixing me, was it a dream?'

Every morning there are hundreds of flies on the walls, on the floors. We swat them. I feel like the proverbial white hunter. I try to have a truce with them, 'You can have the walls but leave my body alone.' No way, they crawl up my legs, land on my face, I hide under the filthy grey blanket, they sneak in, no mercy. No surrender, I am Paisley, I lash out, jumping on my springs and on my bars. Don't slip, they will get their revenge if I end up with a broken back. I can't go to surgery. Carefully get them: some of them are stunned, I think they are dead, no, they recover. They are like the Provos, unconquerable, they are everywhere, and then the little ones that live in the skirting boards (even though the cells are supposed to be cleaned each time we are moved), hundreds of years of filth are ingrained in the floorboards, thousands of flies live there. And in some of the cells there are fleas. One morning we were changing cells and the screws got into a panic when they were moving the mattresses, hundreds of fleas flew up, the screws ran shrieking out into the wing. The male screws in their weird outfits came along with disinfectant putting it everywhere. The female screws are frightened of the fleas because they will be infected by them and who wants a flea-ridden screw to screw?

13. Health

> A doctor has a special duty to individuals which, in this matter, transcends national interest and security. Doctors having knowledge of any activities covered by the Declaration of Tokyo, have a positive obligation to make those activities publicly known. BMA Code of Medical Ethics, 1979 (quoted in *Beating the Terrorists?* by Peter Taylor)

One of our major preoccupations was our health. Every part of the body that can run down on you, will. My eyes got very painful. My hands were never washed. During the 'decoration' of my cell the substance would get in my hair and no matter how carefully I rubbed the walls with newspaper, the newspapers would always tear and the substance would wander around corners and get onto the fingers and hands. It would dry on your hands and then flake off. This, together with the constant dust and fluff from the blankets, made my eyes always itchy. The light was a dim yellow bulb which strained my sight. My spectacles were never clean; dandruff was always getting onto them. Mucus would gather at the corners of my eyes and I would wake up every morning to find them caked. They would have to be prised open with filthy fingers. Some of the young women found that their eyesight had got bad and they would have to order spectacles: these would take three months. I suffered a lot from my teeth breaking off in bits because of the reverberations when I shouted against the steel doors to communicate with the other cells.

I was most scared about possible vaginal infections, which quite a few suffered from. We never changed our knickers or jeans, but one had to have some protection there. Most of the women wore sanitary towels but there were no sanitary belts, so much of the time in the exercise was spent in furtively hitching the towels into place out of view of the TV monitors. The problem of not washing during menstruation was solved by changing the tampax much more frequently than one would outside. Also I had a period only once while inside, which relieved my problem. In the beginning you could get as many sanitary towels and tampax as you wanted. But then surgery came round and informed us that we were going to get them only on the first day of the month, and you had to choose between tampax or towels. The whole problem of menstruation had been a taboo area, never discussed in the *Republican News*. Eilis once talked in the yard about how the men in the Blocks were becoming educated.

'Some of those wee lads know nothing about periods. One of them was asking, does it come out from a hole, just pouring down? It had to be explained to them. They are beginning to understand what we are going through. The shortage of sanitary towels. They don't know how we stick it.' And so on and on.

While they thought the authorities were indifferent to their appeals for help when their periods were too heavy or too frequent, a new area of sympathy and understanding had been discovered, from the men in the Blocks. Some of the girls said that they preferred too many periods than none at all: 'It is healthier,'—anything to indicate that their bodies would not let them down over the no-wash protest. The closed faces in the yard after we had been weighed indicated those girls that had lost weight again.

There are so many parts of the body to watch: hair (some of them were losing their hair; I found when I was combing my hair that it came away in fistfuls), broken nails, flaking skin: until the cell looked like a rat's nest.

It was impossible not to get the excreta onto the floor. The most difficult part to decorate was the ceiling, we had to balance on the bed-rail and make broad sweeps across the high arched cells. Dried pellets would come down onto one's hair and down one's back.

We sweated all the time, which gave a permanent itch to the skin and a sweet sickly smell to one's T-shirt. My pyjamas, I couldn't face putting them on in the end. I wished we had the freedom of the men in the Blocks who were absolutely naked and not hampered by sodden clothes. The few times we had downpours in the yard, some of the women would gather underneath the drain-pipes to let the water flow down their hair and down their bodies. It meant of course that our clothes got soaked, but it was worth it for those two minutes. There was a bare minimum of food, very seldom did we get fresh vegetables or fruit. Hunger-pangs never left us. I had never expected this feeling of permanent starvation.

One afternoon when we were all locked up in our cells, we heard Rosie N. screaming and screaming. We were the fourth door away from her and Katrina. There were hurried footsteps as screws ran to her cell. We tapped on Eilis and Ann-Marie's pipes, they tapped on Ann and Noreen's, who were being visited by Fr Murray and were laughing and singing songs. We were blocked from information, we didn't know what was happening, still Rosie N. was screaming. We discovered what had happened when we got out for supper. Katrina was standing up and suddenly fell into a deep faint. Her head and hands were cold, with no feeling. The nurse came and said that she would take a blood sample which she did, but that it would be a few days before they found out what was wrong. She was not transferred to the hospital wing for observation. We were all worried about Katrina, because she had lost a lot of weight and could hardly drag herself around the yard for the full hour.

Another incident. About 2.30 a.m. we heard tapping on the pipes. It was Rosie C. She whispered, 'Send for the night-guard.'

We whispered, 'Why?' We heard nothing; then we heard crying; we shouted for Margaret, then no sound at all. I rang and rang for the night-guard. We didn't know what was happening, the lights in the cells had been switched off. We heard the night-guard going away and then coming quickly back. We couldn't hear Margaret, but we heard the guard saying to Rosie C. 'Drink this.' She had to put a straw through the spy, because she did not have the keys—there was no possibility for the cell to be unlocked quickly in an emergency after the day-screws had left. When the guard went away we tapped again to Rosie C. They had heard a loud rustle amongst the paper in their cell: they were terrified, they couldn't see, they thought it was a mouse, they couldn't even shout or get out of bed. When the guard turned the light on they found it was a large bluebottle trapped in the paper.

Maria once whispered through the spy to Shirley that she was bleeding black blood from her back passage. She told the nurse, who dismissed the matter and told her that there was no worry as long as it was not black. 'But it *is* black,' she said. 'Oh, that's different,' said the nurse and went away. Maria looked thin and haggard but cheerful. We would look at her and let our imagination work. We were most worried about not having access to the women in case of a medical emergency—especially, as in the case of Maria, when we could only meet at Mass on Sundays. Eileen began vomiting as well as having asthma. In the beginning she was in our group at exercise times; but halfway through her sickness the group was changed. Then we could see her worried thin face only when we whispered through the spy. 'Have they told you what's wrong with you?' 'No, they're just waiting.'

Mary was vomiting and had diarrhoea, then Shirley had it. Was there going to be an epidemic? They were not out in the yard, which meant they must be too weak. When they did emerge, they were thinner and feebler, but were not given any extra nourishment to make it up. Surely the world would alert itself to what was happening? At times they appeared like children in a nightmare, wanting their mothers to wake them up and say it was over. Half of them could not accept the blatant vindictiveness. If only they could be heard, they thought, then surely the British government would understand.

Of course the North of Ireland authorities were concerned that no major disease or epidemic should break out which would result in death. But they were also using the girls' fear of their bodies breaking down as a form of pressure to get them off the no-wash protest. This was well understood by the prisoners, who, even so, lived on the hope that they would get their political status, with all their remission back, so that they could return to the world while they were still of a child-bearing age. Very few women in UK jails ever serve more than 10 years and yet some of these young women like Dolours Price, Ann Bates, and Dolores O'Neill were going to be there for 20 years or for ever, Mairead—14 years, Sinead—12 years.

14. Control of Bodies

'Women must control their own bodies' is the most important feminist slogan; and when one understands the lack of control over their bodies by the women in Armagh Jail, the reason for its importance becomes only too clear. At times I fantasised that we were part of some ancient matriarchal tribe with Mairead as our Inkosi-kaas; but in the area of medicine and healing there was no expert knowledge available except that provided by the British government. This was the potential crack in our solidarity that the authorities presumably hoped would open and widen until it finally broke the protest. If the government did not know what was happening to the bodies of the young women, they should never have taken the responsibility of jailing them, so many in the one place for such long sentences; if on the other hand they are well aware of this, then I can only think that they are deliberately conducting a controlled experiment in psychological and physiological deprivation.

Has the British Medical Association considered the implications of their members in the prison service having to work with such a system in the name of humane care? Has it considered, for example, the lack of trust between doctor and patient that must inevitably develop under such conditions; particularly if the patient is deliberately taking part in a politically-motivated protest against the system, and the doctor is an official of that system? In order to protect its power and privileges in a scientifically-ignorant society, the medical profession tends anyway to shroud itself in mystery. In particular it will do this in relation to the working classes, and, within the working classes, primarily the women. How much more so, then, when the patients are not only working-class women, but also prisoners, and not only ordinary prisoners but ones with whose cause the doctor cannot necessarily be expected to feel sympathy? The women in Armagh, through fear or lack of knowledge, felt themselves totally dependent upon the medical authorities: and yet were aware of these not only as healers but also as members of the authority whom they defied. Thus monstrous patriarchal figures were born in their imagination – Bluebeards, Jack-the-Rippers.

The British propaganda is that the northern Irish jails are the most humane in Europe. But Humphrey Atkins, in a statement delivered in the House of Commons on 30 June 1981 (trying to show his acknowledgement of the Strasburg human rights criticism of inflexibility by government regarding the jails) said that prisons are best run where there is a degree of 'mutual tolerance and acceptance between staff and inmates'. When I was in Armagh, however, before the Strasburg pronouncement had made its impact, the inflexibility was only too apparent in the medical treatment of the women.

For example: one woman had been inside, with political status, for three years. She complained of pains in her stomach. As soon as she was released, she was rushed to the Royal Victoria Hospital where she underwent an emergency operation for a perforated duodenal ulcer, and was put on a special non-greasy diet. Before she had time for her final check-up in the hospital, she was re-arrested, and put back into Armagh, where of course she no longer had political status. She joined the protest: and it took two years for the Northern Ireland Office to provide her with her special diet, after she had again complained of the recurrence of her ulcers.

Another woman had very bad sinus trouble. Under the eyes her face was black and blue with bruises, and she had difficulty in breathing properly. She was grossly underweight. An outside consultant recommended she should have an operation. But the

Northern Ireland Office said that eight screws must guard her if she were to be taken to an outside hospital. The prison was under-staffed; so she was faced with an indefinite wait. Stalemate.

A similar case was that of a prisoner who suffered from lumps in her breast. She did not understand what was causing these: but she was told she should have an operation. Once again, no available staff to take her.

Most frightening of all was the ever-present spectacle of Pauline McLaughlin. When I was in Armagh she was only five stones in weight. A nineteen-year old girl who looked like an old woman of ninety. Hair falling out, teeth falling out, emaciated skeleton-body like something out of the Belsen records. She could not keep her food down. More than once she collapsed and was taken as an emergency case to an outside hospital where she had fluid pumped into her. She was then treated inside the hospital: the only place they were able to insert the needle into her was her heel because the rest of her flesh was so appallingly reduced. Many protests had taken place and articles had been written about her case, but at the time I was there the authorities consistently maintained that she was in control of her own condition, and that she could only be expected to get better if she came off the protest. Happily for Pauline the agitation outside grew, during the autumn, into a momentous campaign. Questions were asked in the House of Lords; Lord Gifford came over to Ireland to have talks with the authorities: and the day after the first hunger strikes ended (December 1980) she was released – conditionally – because of fears of her imminent death.

We thought that her continued presence in the prison in such a state was being used as a warning to us all – a scapegoat, a scare-crow, set up with cold callous calculation to let prisoners know how they would end up if they remained on the protest. Was it any wonder then that we poured our scorn on the medical profession? The women were not amenable to excuses as to why treatment for their own complaints was not immediately forthcoming; for time was running out, the body – once damaged – how could it repair itself in these conditions? – acne, urinary infections, vaginal in-fections, digestive troubles – they did not receive the heavy-handed male medical jokes in the spirit with which they were presumably offered – of reassurance and jollying-along. 'Honey-moon disease', 'get pregnant to clear up your skin', 'nerves: your mind is fighting your body' etcetera. The implication of these comments was that women are physically and mentally too weak to defy the government, and therefore they should give in, respond like 'ordinary women criminals' and avail themselves of the selection of tranquillisers and such-like always ready in the surgery. This was all part and parcel of the archaic nineteenth-century paternalism of the north of Ireland: the same attitudes adopted by the medical authorities seventy years ago in England, when the suffragettes were on hunger strike for the right to vote.

The republican women, however, refuse to take the drugs. They prefer to be fully conscious of what is going on, even though it means their own death.

15.   Church

The Starless Sky

> The sky is starless tonight,
> Or so it seems from my cell window.
> One little patch of sky is better than none,
> So I suppose I should be grateful,
> Or should I?
> Should be grateful for the little things
> That have been pressed upon me
> By the oppressors of our land.
> The little things that grow and grow,
> Until nothing is left
> But the freedom of my soul.
> But a flame burns within me,
> So strong,
> Not even my enemies will quench it,
> Never ending,
> Until the day my country is free.

Christine Beatty (Armagh prisoner)

The Church hierarchy in Northern Ireland is in a dilemma. On the one hand it is used, as it always has been used, by the British government to exert control over the catholic people. On the other hand the Church cannot survive without the people; and the independence of young people, in particular those who have embraced the Republican Movement, has presented a considerable threat. The dilemma was felt acutely in Armagh.

The jail was in the Cardinal's own parish: the prisoners were his immediate pastoral responsibility. If he ignored them he would lose them and their supporters outside. He occasionally paid a visit. Once, after 7 February, when he discovered the screws were not feeding the prisoners, he insisted that they be fed. He threw cigarettes into the cells, wished the girls the best of luck, and departed. Five priests from the Parish House would say Mass in the prison in turn. The prison chaplain, Fr Murray, was an outspoken and fearless champion of justice. Did the Cardinal allow Fr Murray to continue his ministrations knowing that he would not remain silent, but at the same time remaining confident in his doctrinal orthodoxy? The women inside felt strongly that the Cardinal's priority was to keep the predominance of the Church.

The prison authorities were ambiguous in their attitude towards Fr Murray. On every occasion possible the screws would show their lack of respect, calling him *Mister* Murray, or at any time whipping up a pretext for not allowing him in. Likewise, in the Kesh, Fr Faul had a difficult time. Now and then the prison authorities would declare that he was guilty of smuggling in some trivial item like a pen, and stop his visits. But then there would be the outcry from *The Irish News*: 'Sectarian penal laws are back!' The religion itself was used as a political counter; from time to time there would be a new move on the board. We would be searched on the way to Mass. Then we would all refuse to go to Mass, then there would be the statements once more to the world: 'The penal laws are back again'; 'Girls not allowed to go to Mass'; and so on.

This insecurity about going to Mass led the girls to develop their own private devotions which the authorities could never interfere with. I once asked in the yard how many of them prayed for political status in the Novenas. To my astonishment not one of them used the prayers for this purpose. I had put this question to a particularly religious girl: she said that she had more important things to pray for. Another one said, 'We will get political status when we have suffered enough.' She did not mean 'suffering for her crimes', but that the degree of their suffering would create the understanding of their position throughout the world. It is just the same in the Block. The men retain humanity and dignity by the use of prayer; the collective saying of the Rosary in Irish strengthens them.

I would listen carefully to the Sunday sermons, and storm in the yard complaining about them. My companions would say, 'We never listen to them; you're the only one who pays any attention; you are not a catholic; it doesn't matter.' A couple of middle-aged women from the Legion of Mary used to come in on Saturday mornings to say the Rosary in the chapel with the girls. They were pro-establishment and not many of the girls wanted to say the Rosary with them. They begged the girls to come, saying that if there were not sufficient numbers, the Governor would stop them coming. The girls took pity on them and a few would attend.

16. Choice of Words

> I am one of many who would die for my country. I believe in fighting the fight to the end. If death is the only way, I am prepared to die. Inscription on a cell wall in Armagh Jail

> I'll wear no convict uniform nor meekly serve my time
> That Britain might brand Ireland's fight eight hundred years of crime

The singing of the rebel songs binds us together as we yell out behind our closed doors, and we know that in so many other places the Irish rebels are singing such songs together—in the Kesh, in Portlaoise, Limerick and the jails in Britain, and in clubs and gatherings of Irish people all over the world. For a time at least the sentimental ballads create the simple sense of unity. In the jails we believe in the essential truth of the songs all the time. It is a belief the British government needs to break, for it is what make for the remarkable strength of the no-wash protest. It is what brought me into Armagh Jail—after singing outside:

> If we could we surely would
> Stand where our militant sisters stood.

St John says, 'In the beginning was the word.' I believe in the word and that there can be no going back on the word once you have really committed yourself to its truth.

At the same time I did find it hard to commit myself thoroughly to solidarity. Outside, when there were disagreements or contradictions, one retreats into one's self. I hate freely, I despise my opponent, I avoid the people I dislike, I cut myself off from them. But here in jail, whatever my feelings, I had to overcome them and still give out my love. Time and again after conversations during the exercise hour, I'd return to my cell, rage eating me up inside. Only by being able to write my diary could I spill off my frustration, and work my way to an understanding of the young women's position. Normally in the outside world no such demands are made of me. I have my family and I can quarrel with them. I love them, I am responsible for them, who else can love them as I do? After all, I have lived their whole history—conception, pregnancy, birth, childhood, adolescence. But in gaol I had only three months to get to know the women and then only a few of them, and only one hour a day to enter into their experience.

In the beginning I valued my solitary existence, the time to think of myself. I could have spent the whole three months on that, but I had to make an effort, summon up enough energy to reach out to the others. At times I open doors blindly, not knowing whether I am just about to step into turbulent and dangerous situations. But unless I do that, would I not be responsible for reinforcing the 'institutionalising' process they all feared would overtake them? I had been there about six weeks (only seven weeks left) when I decided for the first time to open such a door.

I normally walked round the yard with a particular pair. We would talk about food, life outside, bars, drinks; they were always talking about the great drinking they used to do outside.

'I would drink about two bottles of vodka a day, I drank in the morning, I drank at lunchtime, I drank again in the evening. I would have been in the AA if I hadn't come in here. My mother would have put me in the AA. I never ate, only chicken and steak when I came home from work. I always held my drink well.'

How much of this was I to believe? We were all laughing as we walked around the yard. But when I returned to my cell I began to think over the conversation. Was it true? I knew how easy it was to slip into the habit of drinking, especially in Belfast where the tensions are so enormous. Maybe they drank because they were nervous about being volunteers. There were always complaints about the number of young people hanging around the clubs drinking and waiting. Maybe they drank because they felt that any day they could be blown to bits, or perhaps caught and have to spend years in jail. But would not their drinking mean that they never did any political work? They were just like ordinary soldiers boozing in the barracks. I churned it over in my mind and thought it had been wrong of me to accept these stories without comment. Were they true or were they not? Normally the yard is kept for trivial yarns, it's the time to get together, chatter and gossip. If this was to be a real opportunity for talking, of getting to know the women, shouldn't I take on a more serious role? Not to could mean that I would leave Armagh and really never know nor understand them. I decided that I would take them up the next day in the yard. I did. 'I was puzzled by what you told me yesterday. If you drank so much and were nearly alcoholics, how could you take the political struggle seriously? When did you ever have time to go to meetings?'

Like a flash, they reared up. How dare I assume that they were not political? A lot of the activities they couldn't tell me about anyway; they never allowed their drink to interfere with their work for the struggle. Suddenly I was facing two revolutionaries, gone were the wee girls now, they were young warriors, I had stumbled into an amazon camp and put the wrong questions. They were committed at all times, they would leave work if it were required. Tears were springing into their young eyes; I had betrayed them by not giving them enough trust and understanding. They were serious. I decided that now I had got them so angry, I would persist.

'But political meetings,' I said, 'they are important?'

'I do go to political meetings, I study Eire Nua, we had classes, you always jump to conclusions.'

I had become the enemy. Every insult that British propaganda had ever brought out was reflected on their faces, and I was British propaganda. I felt I had uncovered a depth of feeling that I had never experienced before in anyone; and that I had let loose so much hostility that my warm relationships were going to be destroyed for ever. The next time they ignored me and I sat with some others. Mairead was there and she came up to me and said that there had been complaints against me, that I was trying to make out that the IRA was nothing but a bunch of alcoholics.

I denied this and said, 'What was I to believe if they said that they were alcoholics? I had to make sure. How was I to know whether they were serious, with all the slagging, different humours and different customs? I had to know. I thought it was a joke, but then I wondered. Is it wrong of me to make sure, how would I ever have got to know any of them unless I questioned what I didn't understand?'

That was the wrong thing to say. Why did I question? What did I want to discover? Grim faces looked at me.

'I'm here only for three months, I want to get to know you.'

'You mean you ask questions because you want to get to know us as individuals?'

'Yes', I said. 'I'm sick of all this 'wee girls' stuff. I have the opportunity to get to know you, some of you, only once a day, how am I going to develop any relationships with you? We can joke and slag till the cows come home, but it doesn't mean anything.'

One of them paused and looked at me. Was her suspicion lifting? Or was I going to be branded as a spy?

'Yes, I'm clumsy,' I said, 'but that is how a lot of relationships are at the start.'

Slowly she said: 'It is difficult for you here. We all know each other and know everything there is to know about each other after four years. But we don't know you. You must understand that we have got to protect ourselves.'

But the other two were still very hurt. On my way in, I stopped at the peep-hole of one of them and said that I was very sorry for hurting her feelings: I just hadn't realised she was joking. I could see her tiny grey figure, standing up facing me in the dark cavern, the shit on the walls, the general filth, the grey blankets, the pot smeared and crusted with shit.

She didn't smile, just said, 'I hope you understand that I am not an alcoholic.' I wasn't able to see the other one to explain to her, but the next day she came to my side.

'We can't afford to quarrel in here, or to keep our hurt for a long time; we're all together and get our strength from each other,' she said. And smiled.

I nearly wept with joy: after casting me out of the strange amazon tribe they were taking me back. My heart lifted, I lay on my bed and was happy.

I suppose it was my isolation, also my growing frustration—at times we appeared totally becalmed, each one of us hiding away in dark holes. Who was in charge? Was it part of a crazy master-plan by the Brits? One day not long after the 'alcoholism' issue, Sile came to me to say that there was a woman from New York visiting the prison, sent by the British Information Service, who said she was a great friend of mine. My heart leapt. My God, what was going on? Who was this woman? Did I know her, Sile asked. She was not looking at me in an accusatory way. I said, 'What kind of woman is she?' My mind went blank, who the hell was she? Suddenly it all clicked, it must have been the woman at the British Information Service I rang up in New York, when I was working with Mary Anderson (one of the founder-members of the Women's Movement in Dublin) to prepare a short article for *Ms* magazine about the Armagh prisoners. Mary had wondered what 'detention at the Secretary of State's pleasure' meant, and I had rung up and given my name. The next day the phone rang, it was the woman calling me back to tell me she had asked her daughter, who was a lawyer, what it meant, but she couldn't answer the question, so they had rung London to find out and would ring back. I had not been hostile to her, merely professional. The next day she rang back to say that London hadn't known. I was now being punished for a short telephone call from East 11th Street (where I was staying between B and C Avenues amongst the Puerto Rican junkies, dropouts and mafia).

'I'm sure she's only saying it to make trouble between me and the other prisoners. If she's such a friend of mine, why hasn't she asked to see me?'

Sile nodded. 'The Brits are clever, they will use any method to breed suspicion.'

Were the British so worried that they had to fly someone over from New York to see Armagh for themselves? In a way I felt encouraged. It must mean that they were becoming alarmed by American pressure. But the prisoners must have felt suspicious. What could they make of me? A perfect Kitsonian caricature, proclaiming Women's Lib; an alleged playwright speaking with a not very definable accent; I didn't come from the North, and yet I could apparently fly here, there and everywhere. My world, my standards and values, were incomprehensible to them. What was I doing in here, a middle-aged woman with four sons and a husband; and yet I appeared to be fancy-free?

One day in the yard, we were lying sprawled on the gravel talking about how uncomfortable the conditions were. One of them said, 'Just being in jail is bad enough—if I could get out by my mother paying a fine for me, I would.' One of them laughed. I decided to take her up. So, my not paying the fine was incomprehensible to them. They could understand my coming in to show my solidarity with them, but they hadn't understood that, like them, I'd had no choice.

I got huffy: 'If you wanted to get off the protest you could, by accepting criminalisation,' I said. 'In what way is my action any different? If I pay the fine, I would be accepting the British crown's right to call me a criminal and I would be paying them into the bargain for calling me one. That has been the great weakness of the North of Ireland, you don't understand politics. If your mother paid a fine for you she would be collaborating with the British authorities.'

Had I made the point, had they understood? Or was a consensus reached that they would respect what I got annoyed about and what I felt was important to me?

Were we not in fact sparring with each other? They were a forgotten tribe held together in this hostile environment, secretly in the thrall of some tyrant of the forest, and I was an explorer who had stumbled in on their strange customs. Just because we spoke the same language didn't mean that we heard the same words. When I first came in, they asked me what I thought of the place. What was I to say? They looked so expectant, their faces turned towards me. I could not express what I felt, it was too new, too confusing. I hadn't sorted out my own reactions to the situation, so I quipped in a sardonic way, 'a holiday camp.' As a dramatist I thought of the holiday-camp image as a sort of Joe Orton bad joke. They didn't comment: they laughed. But much later on, it was thrown up to me reproachfully that I had said that. 'Holiday camp' to these young women meant an escape from the ghetto, Butlins, Benidorm, young men, happiness, gaiety. So even though we appeared to be light-hearted and free, when we went back to our cells the brooding and suspicion obviously grew, every word I'd said was mulled over and remembered.

It was good for me to have to choose my words carefully, and also to remember the vast cultural differences between us. All the same, the fact that the surface agreement was broken and that we could argue over our differences in the yard meant that there was some form of understanding and coming together.

Why should they have bothered to take so much trouble to make me feel relaxed? After all I was not in the Republican Movement, I was not from Belfast, they could have ignored me. Was it because they understood that if I was unhappy and isolated, I might break down, pay my fine, and get out and give all the wrong stories once I was home? I don't think so. Having been accepted on the no-wash protest, I was in with them, all of us together. There could be no weak links.

They could have refused to accept me in the beginning. The flexibility of the Republican Movement is never really understood. There is none of the hectoring style, the laying down of pure dogma normally associated with the left. Republicanism seeps into people's consciousness because of the pervasive reality of the British presence in the six Counties. It is as organic a part of a family's way of life as catholicism. The extent of change from armchair republicanism into activism depends upon the comparative behaviour of the British Army and the RUC in each area.

17. Hunger Strike

I see Bernadette Devlin has said that if we were Judith Todd being force-fed in S. Africa or a Russian Jew or a political prisoner in any other country, then the British press and MPs would be screaming. It's quite true, the whole time that Russian author was on hunger strike we were getting hourly reports on him on the radio, and he was sitting in the comfort of his own flat all the time, and although we had started our hunger strike just before him there wasn't a word about us. I take it the English people are only concerned about a person's life if they agree with his or her politics—such hypocrisy makes me sick! Letter from Dolours Price on hunger strike 1974

He has chosen death:
Refusing to eat or drink, that he may bring
Disgrace upon me; for there is a custom,
An old and foolish custom, that if a man
Be wronged, or think that he is wronged, and starve
Upon another's threshold till he die,
The common people, for all time to come,
Will raise a heavy cry against that threshold,
Even though it be the King's. . . .
While he is lying there,
Perishing there, my good name in the world
Is perishing also. I cannot give way,
Because I am King; because, if I give way,
My nobles would call me a weakling, and, it may be,
The very throne be shaken.

from W. B. Yeats: *The King's Threshold*

Martin Meehan began his hunger strike in May, a few days after I came into Armagh. The sole evidence for his conviction on a charge of kidnapping was an informer's statement. A taxi-driver, who could have provided Meehan's alibi, was not allowed to give evidence. He was sentenced to twelve years. All along he had asserted that he had been framed and he went on hunger strike to get his appeal heard sooner than the scheduled date of October. Another young man, Seamus Mullen, had also been convicted—of blackmail; he too said he was framed. He was a member of the IRSP. I had not followed the trials too closely as I had been in New York, but the prospect of hunger strikes starting while I was in Armagh was alarming: they would have terrible repercussions inside the jail. Both men swore that they would die rather than give in.

In the beginning Martin Meehan's hunger strike made very little impact. It was an individual action. The Republican Movement disapproved and had in fact ordered him off, but he ignored them. One of the young women who came from Ardoyne knew him and was upset. *The Irish News* gave no information. About mid-June advertisements began appearing there, put in by the Meehan family, giving some information, but there was no real news or radio or print. By the beginning of July, more ads began appearing, signed by organisations, but still no coverage in *The Irish News*. It was never discussed in the yard. Then one day a meeting was called, to announce that the Republican Movement had decided to support Martin Meehan's hunger strike. It was explained that they had neither encouraged it nor approved of it, but he was determined to go through with it, they would support his individual right. Bernadette McAliskey had gone into the jail to see him: and came out with a statement, that he was doing it on behalf of all prisoners in Northern Ireland who had gone through the farcical Diplock Courts. Support committees were now springing up in Derry, Ardoyne, and the Falls Road; and these linked Seamus Mallon's hunger strike with Meehan's.

At the same time the courts were passing sentences of astonishing leniency upon loyalists, which added fuel to the flame. For instance, there was a two-year suspended sentence for a man who had helped his son (an RUC man) kidnap a priest and had also hidden the gun with which the same son had arbitrarily shot a catholic. *The Irish News* was full of letters from Fr Faul and others, pointing out these injustices.

Inside the jail on the daily exercise hour we would discuss the implications of Martin Meehan's hunger strike: 'He's too proud, he can't take it; just because he's Martin Meehan, he can't stand being locked up, he's only doing it for himself; he's breaking the solidarity; why couldn't he have waited till the autumn? It's not fair to the other prisoners; if he dies they will all have to go on hunger strike and they're not ready for it, he's selfish and it's bad for the young ones in there; they've always looked to Martin Meehan, he's a hero; he's been ordered off and he's disobeyed orders, he's setting a bad example. Any young fellow can think he can do it alone, he can't get anywhere with it; no way, are they going to change the courts just for him? He knew the appeal was coming up in October, he could have waited until after his appeal . . .' and so on.

I tried to present Martin Meehan's point of view, but arguing with any northerner is something which only the bravest should try. I thought, if only the left were here! How well they would have recognised all the arguments. I wondered if there was not an element of self-preservation in them too. After all if Meehan died, we would all have to go on hunger strike and with all the worry about weight-loss, how long could they survive? I brought this up, a bad mistake. Like hissing snakes they all attacked me. Any suggestion, at any time, that criticising a comrade might be based on self-interest was dismissed at once, no way. They were frightened, and no wonder. The whole protest, so apparently solid, could easily crumble if undermined by erratic individualism. But I was thinking in political terms, of the general effect on the nationalist community. Martin Meehan was, I assumed, an experienced campaigner who knew what he was doing.

Round and round we debated. If it seemed that I was attacking Martin Meehan, they in turn hissed back at me. 'You don't understand, we're all solid, in the face of criticism from the outside world we will give him full support.' When he escalated his hunger strike into a hunger-and-thirst strike (after the government had implied that he had been furtively eating) there was no more bickering amongst us: just total support.

Then the Cardinal and Bishop Daly somehow persuaded him to give up the hunger strike. There was tremendous and genuine relief when we realised he was not going to die.

18. Business In The Yard

> If they hadn't brought in the steam cleaning, they would
> have had to give way on the Special Category because the
> medical people were on the point of closing the whole
> thing down as a health hazard. A member of the Prison
> Officers' Association (Long Kesh)

> We protested for equality,
> You battered us.
> We protested for justice,
> You interned us.
> We protested for freedom,
> You murdered us.
> Did you not know,
> You were strengthening the revolution?

> From *The Fruits of Revolution*, 'Gerry' (H Block prisoner)

The details of IRA activities were one area never discussed and I
never asked. Which is not to say that I was not curious. The reply,
quite correctly, would have been if I wanted to know, I could join;
if I just wanted information I must be a spy. The other area that was
never discussed was the charges, and what they felt about the
consequences of their actions.

The republican prisoners remained unaffected by the intense
battery of moralistic propaganda insisting that they should feel
guilty for their crimes. They were fighting a war. Simply that. At
times indeed the atmosphere was like a soldiers' barracks; no
intense conversation, no debates about military strategy. My life-
style outside is one of polemic; I'm inclined to rush out onto the
street and engage any passer-by who can spare the time with a
burning debate on the issues of the day. With my cell-mate this was
not appropriate, so I tended to use the exercise yard for this activity.
Once or twice I thought it might be good for us to exercise our brains
on what kind of military defence we should have in a new Ireland. It
was something they had never thought of (nor had I until that
moment) though it was certainly something a revolutionary party in

a small country such as ours should occasionally ponder. What use would we have for a conventional army when squeezed in by America and Britain with their nuclear weapons? When I first suggested the possibility of alternative strategies, there was an outcry. Then one of the younger women saw my point and began to get very interested. I felt that as I was in a revolutionary prisoner-of-war camp I should keep reminding them of their roles as freedom-fighters and of my role as the only civilian there. I alone represented the 'plain people of Ireland'. We didn't really come up with anything great, but certainly the old-fashioned method of relying solely upon killing people with bombs and guns hardly seemed revolutionary.

The one subject upon which we all exercised our brains was the negotiations on prison conditions between the Cardinal and Secretary of State for Northern Ireland, Atkins: negotiations that had started as a gesture to the Commission on Human Rights in Strasburg, and which the women knew were doomed from the start; though I thought that a large number of promising developments in fact were taking place, in particular inside the British Labour Party. Wedgewood Benn signed Charter Eighty, and the National Executive Committee produced a paper of recommendations about the reform of the entire penal system, based on the prisoners' five demands. *The Irish News* was constantly mulled over and so were the regular radio bulletins that Jennifer shouted across from B Wing.

During my period in Armagh, the verdict of the European Commission on Human Rights was published, stating that the British Government were not guilty of torture in the H Blocks, but had shown rigidity and vindictiveness towards the prisoners. A couple of weeks prior to this announcement, a meeting had been held in the yard to discuss the new concessions from the British Government. The concessions were that we were to be allowed a food parcel, consisting of ½lb of chocolate, 4 lbs of fruit and 100 cigarettes, plus an extra visit each month. These were offered with no strings attached and as far as I know the offer still stands. Everyone knew immediately why the concessions were being given: it was the result of international pressure. They also knew that they were in fact as insulting as the 'concession' allowing the men in H

Block to wear shorts at exercise. The men in H Block however had not been offered the food-parcel and visits. The tactic was meant to divide us. A hundred cigarettes meant just three a day and we were getting that anyway. There was very little discussion before we rejected them. As Mairead pointed out, the British government was making the offer without demanding any concessions from us: so if they could do it on this issue, in the end they could do it for all the five demands.

Three other concessions were offered while I was there. At the first meeting I attended we were told the North of Ireland Office was offering us three clean blankets, sheets, and bedspreads. This was after four months of the no-wash protest. The sheet offer was thrown out immediately, as there was no advantage to us in clean sheets that would only get dirty very quickly—particularly as it was not stated how often the sheets would be changed. It would only serve to make a propaganda point for the British government. During this meeting I felt unable to offer an opinion, as I had been in too short a time.

On the question of the clean blankets there was a lot of discussion. It was debated from all sides. If we rejected everything, would we ever gain anything? Or if we accepted everything, how much propaganda would the British gain out of it? It was decided that they couldn't really make any capital out of clean blankets. It was for health and hygenic reasons as much as for anything else. There was a real possibility of lice and fleas breeding. The existing blankets by this time were filthy. The Governor had removed the sheets and pillow-cases following the 7 February attack. There seemed to be no point in rejecting the blankets; because they were not a 'concession'—it was to the government's interest to keep us healthy. So one day our old mattresses, pillows, and blankets were all thrown out to be burnt and we got a clean mattress, three very dark, heavy, grey blankets (more like horsehair) and two pillows. Mine were stuffed with straw.

The second meeting I attended dealt with Mairead's longstanding negotiations with the Governor about our exercise hours. She wanted us all to be allowed out at the same time. She also felt that the 10 o'clock exercise time was at too early an hour, and a lot of the women didn't come out on it. This was because of the very long breakfast procedure. You had just returned to your cell to sit down and drink your tea when you had to go out to the yard. Once again, whose was the advantage? The Governor agreed to let 16 of us out from 10.30 to 11.30. On the one hand we knew that it made life easier for the screws just to have 1 hour of exercise in the morning and afternoon instead of 4 hours altogether. It also meant that we were losing 2 hours a day collectively. Couldn't we get 1½ hours instead? Or would this make the British government appear too humane? But 16 people all let out at once meant that they were being given political association—at least for half the Company at a time—which was to our benefit. Mairead decided to accept the 16-at-a-time arrangements but would continue to negotiate for the 1½ hours for all of us. This innovation made everyone very excited because there had been no opportunity to see some of their comrades since 7 February (except on Sundays, when we had no time to talk).

I was very impressed by the way these meetings were conducted. There was time and confidence for everyone to put their viewpoints before the vote was taken. Mairead guided them into seeing the problem from all angles and it was dealt with in a very practical way. She was determined that our living conditions should not be subject to decisions taken out of extremist romanticism, or the desire to make an empty gesture.

The Governor himself must have been impressed by this calm, intelligent young woman as she pointed out to him how much it was to his advantage to deal with her as C.O. It saved a lot of trouble. How could he otherwise enforce anything when these women were so solid in their unity? Also he must have known that not one of the girls respected him after his firm stand on 7 February had turned into what became known throughout the country as 'The Hospital Riot'. Although he would never publicly declare that he had no control or authority inside A Wing, we felt he absolutely relied on this young woman. The day before I was released Mairead won her demand for all the women to be allowed out on exercise together twice a day.

There were other meetings, some to do with IRA business. As I was not a member of A Wing Company, I did not attend these, but used to go jogging while they met in one corner of the yard, trying to avoid the watchful eye of the TV monitor. The screws would be sitting in their little glass huts staring impassively ahead like dummies in a shop window or chatting to each other. If the sun was out they would bring out their chairs and sit with their backs to the walls, sunning themselves, their walkie-talkies strapped to their waists. Prisoners and screws never made any sign of recognition to each other at any time during the exercise period. Occasionally the Governor and the head screw would come through the yard for inspection. The screws were supposed to stand up to attention. They would obey, reluctantly: half standing up, either propping themselves up against the hut or propping their leg against the wall.

One day he brought in a new face, it was the Northern Ireland Office's security consultant, who wandered around, looking and pointing about. The reason for this must have been the following incident. One day the male crims, who have an exercise yard adjoining ours, threw a ball over to us. Rounders was quickly organised, but someone landed the ball on top of the workshop where the female crims used to work. How to get the ball down? A human ladder was organised, and up went one girl onto the flat roof. The screws apparently paid no attention; but shortly afterwards the consultant appeared. Then there was a lot of mysterious activity on the roof by uniformed male screws. All was revealed in a short time. Some sort of tree-hut had been erected and there the screws were put, staring impassively out.

Outside our heavy grey stone crumbling walls was the city. Above the far end of the yard there was a little hill with a housing estate and Paisley's church on it. Sometimes there would be weddings, some of the prisoners would stand wistfully watching the wedding-parties pose for their pictures. There were masses of colour in the orderly neat gardens belonging to the prison officers' houses. We could hear the rumble of traffic, especially at night, motor-bikes racing round and round. Apparently this was a social problem in Armagh. *The Irish News* had articles in the middle about the young people in Armagh who do Evel Knievel acts in the middle of the town at midnight to frighten the inhabitants. There were few social amenities for them. Court cases were also reported of drunkenness and fighting in the town. Helicopters would come regularly to patrol the jail.

Round and round we would go, some of us in little groups, some of us individually, we would just walk and walk. Most of the women in the beginning had stout, strong lace-up shoes brought in. They reminded me of new-school-term outdoor shoes. As they paced round and round the young women looked like well-shod ponies. Very few of them had the energy to walk around for the entire hour but would sit huddled on the steps of the jail and out of the wind, not talking very much but sitting together like stray kittens. Because of the weight-loss, the no-wash protest and the prison pallor, their eyes seemed enormous, and their small grey faces peeping out of tangled hair. When they laughed and became animated they were like children. All sexuality had disappeared, even though, when visitors came, they would put on gold ear-rings or little drop ear-rings.

The yard was never the same from day to day; bad news from outside or no letters, or the worsening news from the Block would darken the mood. New babies, weddings, or a visit from a sister would brighten them up.

19. Culture and Controversy

A parallel conference to last week's United Nations sponsored International Women's Convention in Copenhagen, Denmark, was attended by hundreds of women including two members of Sinn Fein: Cathleen Knowles (General Secretary) and Marie Moore (Ard Comhairle) . . . The Dublin-based Armagh Prisoners' Solidarity Committee sent a delegate, free-lance journalist Nell McCafferty. She raised the question of the women political prisoners in Ireland at the forum's press conference: and French journalist Jacqueline Heinen, form *Rouge*, raised the question during the address of Free State Minister Brendan Daly, which created a stir among the press. News item in *Republican News*

Our collective evening entertainment was modelled on the entertainment worked out in the H Blocks. The Entertainment Officer was Christine, who had the job of getting quizzes smuggled in, working them out herself, or inventing games. A few days after we arrived there was a meeting during the exercise period in which Mairead admonished us all for not helping Christine sufficiently. The evening period was the only time we could act collectively. It was also a means of breaking down depression and the tendency to turn inwards. We must all participate by vocally showing that we were together. Mairead said it wasn't fair to Christine, who stood there looking reproachfully at us. 'Were we bored by the entertainment that was offered?' she asked.

I must admit that I had never been very enthusiastic about 'who sang what song on Top-of-the-Pops' somewhere around 1975? I didn't know any of the answers. When I had first been put in Christine's cell, she and Breige were working on the quiz. They asked me to compile a list of 200 novels, their authors and characters. My mind went blank. I could think of authors but not titles and I couldn't think of a single character. I realised what a careless reader I was. I felt very inadequately prepared for a prison where the occupants had been deprived for years of books or any popular entertainment. We should have thought about this before going in. Titles of films, who played what, plots? All I could think of was the latest Russian films I had seen, or the Fassbinder films I had gone to see one wet afternoon on 8th Street New York. But once I made up my mind that I had to throw some energy into it, it was great fun.

They all knew how ignorant I was, and when the questions were yelled at me (I found it very difficult to hear through the heavy doors) the answers would be yelled out at me as well. I would then declaim them as though they were my own and get a mark. We entered into the spirit of the game as seriously as soccer fans, yelling, banging our doors to encourage the competitors, booing if our side was not winning. The games were played in teams, one side of the wing against the other side, sometimes individual cells against each other. I discovered that the book listing was of the popular romances that they had had access to in B Wing— Catherine Cookson, for instance, who had written hundreds.

Fortunately my ignorance was not something that would be noted down and remembered. There was no real competitiveness.

The only game of chance we played was bingo, once a week, with genuine prizes—a roll-up, or occasionally a real cigarette. We were given bingo cards by Christine when we arrived. The card was inked out on an envelope and we made our markers by tearing up tiny pieces of newspaper. I finally won a game after Liz, who seemed to be very lucky, gave me her card when she was released. One evening I won three cigarettes and found I could have become a bingo-addict, so intense was the pleasure when I actually won. But then it was overdone as I won all the prizes that night; everyone was delighted, and jokes were made when I didn't win again after that. I was asked to be a bingo-caller a couple of times.

Mairead took Irish for beginners two nights a week, painstakingly calling out the words and spelling, we would then repeat them over and over again. The next night she would ask us simple questions. I had learnt Irish at school, but for some reason had always resisted it. However in jail I really enjoyed it. Eilis, while she was in the cell next door to me, would give me the words I had missed and I would copy them down and learn them, making up simple sentences. I even began writing letters in Irish to Irish speakers in Galway. The problem was that every Irish word in letters going in or out of the jail was censored. I hit upon a plan that I thought would at least exercise my mind and temperament. Now that the 26 Counties were in the EEC, Irish was officially recognised as an EEC language. It was therefore my official language. In the 26 Counties there is a very militant group of Irish enthusiasts and the government has what are known as special Gaeltacht areas, where families get a grant for speaking and writing Irish as their first language. So I wrote to a couple of these people: first going to Mairead and saying that if my letters didn't get out, we could sue the Northern Ireland Office at the Court of Human Rights for suppressing our EEC-recognised culture. She looked at me in amazement at first. The work of going back and forth to the Governor would be greatly increased for her, burdened as she was by the real issues inside the jail: health, visits, release-dates, etc. But she agreed, and she had a word with Marie who was in charge of communications with the censor. I wrote my letters in Irish, corrected by Mairead, who must have felt a certain pride in seeing the fruit of her labour

To our surprise, the censor said that there was no problem—my letters would be sent out. Alas, no replies came; the letters had never arrived. I could not prove anything. The censor assured Marie that the letters had been sent out. It must have been loyalist post office workers, who saw the Gaelic address and threw them out. Still it kept me busy and entertained.

Some of the women were very good at Irish. They had had classes in B Wing, and had got bored; but now that they were locked up it became a challenge. Many of their comrades in the Kesh had become fluent speakers. We had discussions about speaking it when we got out for our dinner, but we felt too shy. Locked up in one's cell, bellowing it out, was one thing, but trying to converse in it eye-to-eye was different. All my nerves and inferiority complex would return to me.

On another night of the week there were lectures. Liz and I were asked to prepare weekly lectures on the Women's Movement. We decided to do three. I'd never had to prepare written lectures before. I was used to a more informal kind of seminar. I found it hard to have to prepare a reasoned logical argument which had not only to be very clearly thought out, but simple enough to be shouted through the door. Liz had had a good degree from Queen's University and I felt very confident that she would be able to manage. But we moved cells after the first lecture and I had to prepare the other two on my own.

I sweated more over them than I ever did over the dozens of lectures I had given in the spring, when I was in America. It was an enormous challenge. The women had been very excited at the prospect of eleven feminists coming to join them on the no-wash protest; for that is what all the publicity about the Armagh Eleven had stated. Also the publicity of Women Against Imperialism, all our marches, the massive turnout on International Women's Day in 1980, and the International Women's Tribunal in Belfast, with names like Vanessa Redgrave and Frances de la Tour, had made them feel that we were a very intellectual movement. The second day I was in, the whispered voices from the next cell said how shy they were of us, and they wondered if they could talk to us, would they be up to it? A lot of this was slagging, of course. They didn't comment when we told them that only Liz and myself were going to be there and that for personal reasons the others weren't going to be able to make it.

Our first lecture outlined the development of the Women's Movement. Then came the questions. We knew we had been set up. The questions bore no relation to the lecture, but expressed what we already knew to be their prejudices: abortion, lesbianism, why were we men-haters, the Catholic Church. Liz and I were trapped in our cell, running from the window to the spy to keep up with the torrent of questions, Liz at times purple in the face with rage as they baited her. This baiting from the entire wing was of course in our imaginations. We were in fact so far at the top of the wing that those at the bottom couldn't hear at all, and probably only three or four of the women were actually arguing with us. But because we didn't know their voices and faces, and were not familiar with where the voices were coming from, we thought that we were being attacked on all sides.

The lectures began at ten. I suppose ours lasted twenty minutes and then the debate carried on until midnight. A great rousing cheer was given to us at the stroke of twelve, when as usual we all bedded down for the night. The next morning, Christine whispered through the spy, that it had been very good and stimulating and everyone had enjoyed themselves and not to forget to do the next two weeks. The final one with the debate afterwards was in a way the most revealing.

We had laid out the development of the Women's Movement in relation to the other oppressed people of the nineteenth century: the slaves, the colonial people, the workers, national liberation struggles (in all of which women had taken part; though their position had not improved proportionately to their efforts). We said it was necessary to have an autonomous women's movement in Ireland. We pointed out the gains the Women's Movement had made since the 1970s, the legislative changes that had taken place in the 26 Counties, the reasons for the movement's indifference to the national struggle in the North. Women had struggled for Irish independence, and yet when the independent Irish Constitution was brought out in 1937, we were given even fewer rights that we had before independence: we were relegated again to being no more than wives and mothers. The relationship between the National Question and the Women's Movement is still an unsolved problem in all of Ireland. Now with the republican women's resistance to criminalisation, women were able to identify with them and support them.

The break-through of course had been when we were all arrested in 1979 on International Women's Day. Was there not a connection between the prospect of a far more massive demonstration on International Women's Day 1980 (in the event it had been 500 strong) and the Governor's decision to bring in the male screws in February to break the women's protest for political status? This in turn—they must have calculated—would have demoralised the men in the H Blocks and thereby weakened the whole republican struggle in the North. The A Wing women had become the focus.

The response of our audience to this line of argument was not quite what we expected. Some women said that they did not like taking part in the debates because they got too worked up and frustrated. You can't hear and you get very very tired shouting out all the time, so I'm basing my judgement on those few who did debate. What came out was a deep distrust of the Women's Movement. By implication we were saying that the Republican Movement had not recognised their struggle in the jail as having an identity of its own, and that it was no more than a support for the men. They were also of course so few in number—the maximum was 40 compared with 400 in the Blocks. The Women's Movement, both in Ireland and in England, had not originally been interested in them at all.

I felt very torn by the debate in jail. A lot of what they said was true, for where was the Women's Movement in 1976 when these women were rounded up, tortured, and thrown into prison? It was their resistance and their commitment to the ideology of republicanism that had given them the strength to go on the protest. None of the women's groups that had sprung up, like Women Against Imperialism, Women in Ireland (in England), the Armagh Solidarity Group, etc., had ever made any contact with these young women and we were as foreign to them as they were to us. Was it not true that certain elements in those women's groups were not really interested in the prisoners, but were primarily using them to impose their own ideas upon the Republican Movement? Yes, the prisoners had appreciated the three or four times we had come picketing outside the jail, but this was only support similar to that of organisations like Sinn Fein and the RAC, who had worked equally hard for the prisoners. So much work had been going on over the last 16 months (the resolutions at the big women's conferences, struggles to get copy published in *Spare Rib*, insistence by women's anti-imperialist groups on speaking at 'Troops Out' meetings, alliances with third-world anti-imperialist groups, and getting them to accept that Ireland was part of the anti-imperialist struggle); but how could these young women know about it?

We had never opened up channels of communication with them, so that they could have followed the debates, and taken the opportunity of letting their own voices be heard. We had excluded them from the women's struggle and indeed we had been fighting on their behalf without ever asking them if they wanted it. Whereas they were in touch, at least once a week, with the Republican Movement, sending out and receiving regular bulletins. Had we an army? they asked. We sang the 'Women's Army' song outside the jail, and we had sung it inside. We were not going to be trapped into answering that question. Fortunately one of the women began shouting, 'It's not fair, they can't answer that!'

The questions that they asked were questions that had never been discussed in the women's anti-imperialist groups. Here we were facing young republicans who had voluntarily taken up arms against one of the mightiest empires of the last two hundred years, interlocked now with the multi-national western imperialist NATO bloc. (I'm not writing about the ones who were forced onto the Conveyor Belt by the RUC, although, even if they had been mere victims to begin with, they were now fully committed). They wanted to know what stand the Women's Movement took on all this. They of course had been fully informed of all the squabbles that had taken place when the 'women's army' had marched through Armagh in 1980. Middle-aged women of the North had watched agog when lesbians who kissed and cuddled in the coach suddenly walked off because a blanket-man was to address the rally.

The presence of men at the socials had sparked off more rows. I was not there when all this had taken place, but bit by bit the confusion of the Women's Movement was revealed to me. Not in a direct way; they never tried to discredit the Women's Movement in the same way that some have tried to demolish these women's involvement in the Republican Movement.

They stated time and again that there was sexual equality in the Republican Movement. I believed them, but only in so far as individual women could be equal to individual men; but I knew that women as a whole, the women's problems that derived from the social and cultural background, were ignored by republicans. If we had been able to pursue this argument we might have got somewhere; but it was really impossible. Besides, they could not understand political development, they had never had experience of it. They did know however that Sinn Fein had now organised a separate women's group, and that the first women's conference had taken place in the autumn.

We in Women Against Imperialism felt that was because our group had shown up and exposed the weakness of the Republican Movement's attitude to women. Why were there not as many women in the IRA as men? We could never debate this, for the IRA is a secret organisation. If they had spoken about it, it would have meant that they were members of the IRA. Don't forget that the night-guard could hear all our debates, and so could the male guards patrolling the jail outside. If you are a member of the IRA (a proscribed organisation) you can get ten years. Only a handful had actually been convicted of membership. The *Republican News*, which carried indications of social change within the movement, was not allowed into the jail. Only isolated news items, such as demos, or pictures of them, were smuggled in. They did not know that WAI had put up a delegation at the H Block meeting at the Green Briar in Belfast. We'd moved a resolution there, that the women in Armagh should be given the same status in the agitations as the men in H Block, and it was overwhelmingly carried. The fact that we had no hierarchical structure was puzzling to women used to a military organisation. That our battle was the political one of raising consciousness was something from which they could see no direct benefit. We could have pointed out that despite the republican struggle, the British Army was still on the streets of the North.

My arrest and detention in a 'British' jail had caused no outcry in the South. There I was, held hostage by an alien power; and my government did nothing. In spite of Charlie Haughey's commitment to the Arts, he allowed one of his few internationally-known playwrights to lie in this midden. Not even the local H Block Committee in Galway sent me so much as a card . . . Nonetheless (and paranoia apart) I was one of the few artists from the 26 Counties who had actually come up to the North to protest publicly about the lack of humanitarian civil liberties: and here I was, buried.

Here in the North however, I did feel that I was protected and cherished. It became clear to the women, that whilst the Women's Movement was very good at getting out generalised propaganda statements, something basic was missing. To begin with, there were no statements about our presence in jail. To get statements into *The Irish News* the normal practice is to insert a paid ad. WAI did not do this. Nor did they send masses of letters of support. Liz and I got no letters from anyone in WAI for four weeks. We were extremely upset because it showed our vulnerability. We knew of course that hardly any women outside had supported our stand on going in. The women in jail became very solicitous and attentive and fiercely took up the cudgels for us. They were outraged that some of the women who had been arrested with us hadn't even bothered to write. They felt quite upset. This was one of the bitterest lessons that we learned, and they had learnt it four years before, when they came in. In spite of the rhetoric, once you are put in jail, you are forgotten about. The people whom you know quite unconsciously accept the British government's right to withdraw their friends from them; and you are left with just a handful of people who really do care. In all our cases, this handful was chiefly made up of our families. And yet the family is the bastion of the patriarchal system. No wonder the girls found it incomprehensible when we asserted the value of women's solidarity. Where were our sisters from the movement now? I did get letters from one or two of the other women who had been arrested with me, but only from those I had been closest to outside.

During the deafening silence, we had begun to get rumours

about what had been happening inside the WAI. There had been a split over the method to be used to get Ann-Marie's children back from Dublin. Two of my friends had left WAI because they disagreed with the tactics adopted, which involved the Garda Siochana and the High Court. I could not talk to Liz about it, as we no longer shared a cell nor were we out in the yard at the same time. So I had to pour out my frustration and bitterness to some of the other women. They found it all fascinating. This was the first time that they had come up against what is known as political struggle. They wanted to know what all the initials of the groups stood for, and what their aims were. It was an exotic foreign terrain for them. The more isolated I became from my comrades outside, the closer I grew to these women and the more we began to understand our problems together. Our families became our only dependable allies. We shared our letters and our photographs and thus became one large family. Their relatives would ask after me; my friends and family would ask after them. As one of them said, 'I know so-and-so's mother as well as my own and yet I've never seen her.' It is very difficult for those outside to understand this; and to understand how the isolation of the prisoners on the protest reinforces their commitment to the IRA.

20.   **The Last Ditch of the War?**

He didn't look as if he belonged in this world, he was really hyped up, his eyes were glazed and were darting all round, but it was as though he wasn't seeing anything. I could hear crashing all over the house. I thought it was a loyalist death squad . . .

I could hear neighbours outside challenging the gunmen, and one of them answering, 'This is a quick way to kill fenian scum.' I thought we would all be killed. I was lying face down on the floor, unable to see anything, just hearing English voices yelling and screaming. Mrs Moyra Berkery, describing an SAS raid on her Belfast home.

I had now come to realise what I had only known before as a kind of abstract declaration. The Partition of Ireland in 1922 had in fact worked: subsequent generations of republicans born and reared north or south of the Border had intuitively grown up as citizens of separate countries with entirely separate experiences, even though the theory of a united 32-county Ireland was still supposed to direct the political aspirations of all of us. In County Galway I lived in a so-called independent state: but one in which our government, hand-in-hand with the British government, effectively imposed a variety of repressive laws (no less draconian than those in the North), determined that the population should not embrace the northern struggle as their own.

But in the catholic ghettos of the North, there could be no doubt that the struggle was their own: the repressive laws themselves were responsible for the people's militancy. It was a pure gut-reaction from the immediate presence of the British Army and the RUC. I had not experienced this, and yet, here in Armagh Jail, I had inadvertently entered in upon the most intense corner of the battlefield. The British had brought the war into the prisons, and here, they believed, could be the making or breaking of their policy.

In all probability my mind was becoming unhinged, lying in a cell 23 hours a day, the walls covered with excrement and then covered with flies, the bowl of urine under the bed sending up a powerful stench. Lying on my grey blankets, the windows daubed and boarded-up outside, no view, except high up, a triangle of clouds racing past; on the floor thousands and thousands of small flies hopping. Two predatory Roman-Imperialist eagles suddenly block out the light. Beside me on the pillow lies an enormous severed hand. I close my eyes and open them again: the eagles are pigeons, the macabre hand is my own, tucked somehow under my neck. There is no relief from the filth except once again to close my eyes. Opposite—a 21-year old girl doomed to lie there for the next ten years with nothing to read but a Bible. Open my own Bible and words thunder through the cell:

> God is jealous, and the Lord revengeth; the Lord reven-
> geth, and is furious; the Lord will take vengeance on his
> adversaries, and he reserveth wrath for his enemies. The
> Lord is slow to anger and great in power, and will not at
> all acquit the wicked: the Lord hath his way in the
> whirlwind and in the storm, and the clouds are the dust
> of his feet.

Why is it so important for them that we admit ourselves to be criminals? But then, why did the Romans want the Christians to offer incense? The friends of the Christians used to beg them: 'Oh it's nothing, offer it; it's only a meaningless gesture.' But the Christians, by refusing, changed the shape of the whole Roman Empire in the end: and one of the reasons why they were able to hold on was their certainty that their God was the only true one, and changeless. Roman Gods were mutable, according to the demands of political expediency. The British policy in the North of Ireland has shown constant inconsistency. All the parties inside the 32 Counties have done some form of turnabout. The only stance the young prisoners can take is one of resistance to a series of illogical and arbitrary moves. Have the loyalists had this consistency? No, they have floundered about, confused, sometimes proclaiming loudly that they too are POWs: in 1972 a 35-day hunger strike led by republicans (including six women in Armagh), and later joined by a few loyalists, succeeded in achieving political status. But now the loyalists come on and off the blanket like jumping-jacks. Since 1976 there have been many re-alignments and reversals in Irish political life in relation to the National Question—some of them traumatic; but inside the jails the republicans have been constant, their aims absolutely fixed. Present propaganda notwithstanding, the IRA were very slow to publish what was happening in the jails. When political status was removed there was sporadic rioting outside. But that soon died down and the people outside seemed to have forgotten (this was a period of internal splits and fratricide within the Republican Movement and the parties supporting it), but inside, in particular inside Armagh, there was little change.

So why is it so important for the British government to get the political prisoners to accept criminalisation? The whole episode is absurd. If you accept the special circumstances of arrest, special law, torture, no jury, and then accept criminal status, as a criminal you are treated better than any other kind of criminal in the United Kingdom. You then become an 'ordinary decent criminal' even though the crimes you have committed are exactly the same as those of the evil 'subhuman animals' who are on the no-wash protest. You get 50 per cent remission (in the rest of the UK it is only a third) and the jails are not crowded. The work in the women's jail is minimal. They go to the workshops at 8.30, the radio plays constantly, they do a little bit of sewing, talk and smoke cigarettes, then go to classes. But out of 40 republican women prisoners only 8 accepted criminal status (and that for personal reasons). The Republican Movement has always maintained that it fights in the name of the people, the British government has always maintained that there is no support for the Republican Movement; and it tries to use the show-down with the prisoners to prove this.

The prisoners are not trained revolutionaries in the conventional sense; there is no way that the republicans can punish them inside the jails for coming off the protest. So from whence comes the strength, this obstinacy, this certainty that they are right, and that the British government has got iself into a corner that it cannot get out of? The prisoners have done everything in their power to show that in the end their adversaries will destroy themselves. The setting up of the National H Block/Armagh Committee with the five demands, and its repeated defusing of the situation so that Britain could get off the hook without losing face, has not pre-vented the government from blundering on. The steadfastness of the prisoners for their right to be treated as political prisoners has only been reinforced by the pig-headedness of the British govern-ment's policy: 'Surrender or die.' To the outside world with its ever-accommodative array of political parties and attitudes, such steadfastness appears unutterably stupid, while the pig-headedness of weakening imperialism seems so strong that all one can do is compromise with it.

Unable to defeat the IRA outside, the British government has turned the jails into the last ditch of the war. They have failed to get the people in nationalist ghettos to surrender the IRA. The reason is obvious. No political guarantees have ever been given to the nationalists. Yes, the nationalists accept the state's handouts but they don't believe in them as their right; they see them as an accident of history. They cannot finally be bought off with cash, especially now that there is no cash for them nor for anyone else in the North of Ireland. So the hope that sustains the prisoners is not an illusion. If they give up, where do they go? Back to the ghettos and the labour exchange. They of course don't think in those terms and in a way they don't have to: that is for us outside.

I found the prisoners' view of life outside difficult to understand as we went round and round the yard. They would be talking about jobs. Yes, they were happy with the boss, yes they were happy with the money, yes the family living-standards have improved. I used to ask myself, why then do they want to change? But there was an air of unreality about the stories of the good times they used to have, about the clothes, pubs, boyfriends, holidays in Spain. Why were they not like the conventional British working class who do not have the confidence to stand up and demand their full rights even though they have the trade unions and the Labour Party? The young women in Armagh have nothing except their knowledge that they are denied their identity in the North of Ireland state. Is not this the clarity which socialist parties outside all strive for?

An example of the prisoners' clarity: when the Human Rights verdict came out in Strasburg (supporting Britain's stand on removing political status), they were quick to realise that Britain had secured a favourable ruling because Strasburg was convinced that negotiations were still going on with the Cardinal. So the verdict came as no surprise. I tried to point out that Britain had not got off scot-free—Strasburg had said that Britain should not be vengeful in seeking retribution from the prisoners. There was room to manoeuvre. This was seen, and denounced, as my support for the verdict. I was seeing the verdict in a muddled way. Their course of action was now clear. It was they themselves, alone, who had to confront the British government. And they were right, the British government *had* got off the hook by entering into negotiations with the Cardinal, who unwittingly (because of his great concern for a peaceful solution) became used by them, they had got the verdict they wanted. And from now on, the British government were sure that no power would shift them.

I was shortly to be released from Armagh and would not be on the final stages of the expedition on which the travellers would be facing the most dangerous waters of the entire journey. For us on the outside, the question would be: how important is the individual life of each Irish republican prisoner?

The show-down was now, and they were to be the instruments of change. They possess an intelligence born out of observation, and they believe that, by and large, intelligent, logical, rational human beings can see the wood for the trees. They have not had to give up any of the trappings (such as the Catholic Church) that we would see as impediments to logic. Time and again we would break into arguments about this, but their belief in catholicism had nothing to do with the teachings or rules of the hierarchy. They took what they wanted and ignored the rest. They took one element of the ideology—hope—and they clung to it with all their might. They pray to the saints, using the religious magazines to find out how to say the Novenas correctly so their intentions may be answered. These are normally to do with the problems their families have; and they believe the families reap the benefit of their prayers. They draw their strength from their families, letters and visits, and—most important of all—from their comrades in the H Blocks, and together they know that they are fighting a just war.

When Volunteer O'Neill was 'killed in action' (surprised in a Belfast street by the RUC, he had drawn them onto him in order to let his two comrades escape, and was shot dead), they had their normal commemoration parade. Many of them had known the dead man. For two days a couple of them went round the yard during exercise, planning the ceremony. After Mass on Sunday we all assembled, a thin ragged Company. In spite of the confiscation of their black clothes, they had managed to smuggle in black armbands, which were given out. I sat and watched, the only civilian. They carried out the parade as gravely and as solemnly as the ranks at the London Cenotaph on Remembrance Sunday. A decade of the Rosary was said, in Irish; a young woman sang a rebel lament ('The Four Green Fields', I think), her pure voice soaring into the open summer sky above the yard; then the oration was delivered.

What did it mean to me? I was half-amused at this atavistic

nineteenth-century militarist format; but their very seriousness and their complete absorption in the soldierly identity of A Wing Company on parade was also unbearably moving. Behind the prison walls, in defiance of the authorities who were looking on powerless, and in spite of their enforced lack of physical energy, they demonstrated their determination to carry on as volunteers—the very determination that the Governor had tried to break on 7 February. All through history tiny bands of rebellious troops had thus proclaimed their pride within stone walls, barbed wire, stockades, and the boundaries of lands of exile. For this they lay in excrement, urine, and menstrual blood. It was epic. As quickly as it had begun, it was over. They were normal young women once more. I had seen just a flash of their other life. The transformation had taken place; and will take place again. They will never be conquered.

Part Three: Outside

21.   Journey's End: Journey's Beginning

> What is to be done? Shall we feminists record that they are
> inflicting the conditions on themselves in case any
> question of moral dereliction arises against us? The
> menstrual blood on the walls of Armagh prison smells
> to high heaven. Shall we turn our noses up? Nell
> McCafferty, in the *Irish Times* 22 August 1980

13 August 1980. I bade farewell to those tiny warriors locked
behind their steel doors, to find that West Belfast had had a
Massacre of the Innocents that internment-anniversary weekend.
Before departing for their NATO exercises in Europe, the British
Army had left a barbaric calling-card behind: they had taken an
indiscriminate revenge upon the young children celebrating at the
bonfires in the housing estates; they had let loose a point-blank hail
of plastic bullets, killing two youths and injuring about seventy.

I found a young friend Ann-Marie (aged fourteen) lying in the
intensive-care unit of a hospital with a badly-fractured skull. Her
mother, who had been a member of Women Against Imperialism,
was at her bedside. We spoke about the death of Miriam Daly.
More members of the National Smash H Block/Armagh Committee were to be assassinated during the next few weeks. Noel Little
and Ronnie Bunting were shot dead in their beds; Suzanne Bunting
(also of WAI), who was seriously wounded, was to be brought to
the same intensive-care unit as Ann-Marie; so too was Bernadette
McAliskey.

All this was designed to intimidate the people so that they would
not take to the streets in support of the demands of the H Block and
Armagh prisoners. But it did not work; by the end of the summer
they had come out in tens of thousands—supporters who had not
been seen on demos for years; internal rifts had been healed and
factional suspicions cooled. And even in the supposedly apathetic
26 Counties the momentum of the Smash H Block campaign grew

and grew. The Women's Movement in both Britain and Ireland was torn in two.

'Is Armagh a feminist issue?' Nell McCafferty in the *Irish Times* affirmed that it was, and threw down the gauntlet. She had been completely converted to this view when she had attended the UN Women's Conference at Copenhagen in the summer. To her surprise hundreds of women there from Latin America, the Third World, and Europe, were supporting the Armagh prisoners, seeing them as feminists and freedom-fighters. *Scarlet Woman, Spare Rib,* and the *Irish Times* opened their columns to the big debate. At every women's conference in Dublin the issue was raised. It was amazing how many women, calling themselves feminists, closed their eyes, blocked up their ears, and ran to their political parties—Fine Gael, Sinn Fein the Workers' Party, the Irish Labour Party—seeking urgent reassurance in the old patriarchal priorities of the women's needs: 'What about the battered wives? One-parent families? Divorce? Contraception? These are the real women's issues, not trying to overthrow the state.' Leading international American feminists came over: once again the Movement was split. Kate Millett supported the women in Armagh, and was largely ostracised: Betty Friedan never mentioned them and she was worshipped.

The line seemed to be drawn between, on the one hand, a reformist utilitarian kind of feminism, deriving largely from the effects of the last few centuries of capitalism and the need to achieve liberation within its contemporary limits; and, on the other, a more fundamental striving against all manifestations of male-dominated political, cultural and social structure which extends much further back into human history than the beginning of modern industry.

Armagh itself is an enduring symbol of control of men over women which was first brought into Ireland, according to the legends, at some time in the Bronze Age. This city, which today the primatial see of the Christian Church in Ireland, and had once been the royal fort of the ancient celtic kings of Ulster, owes its very name (Ard Macha, in Irish) to the brutal humiliation of the goddess-bride, Macha, who had come to live there with Crunniuc, a nobleman to whom she was attracted. One day he went to the annual fair . . .

'It would be as well not to grow boastful or careless in
anything you say' the woman said to him.
'That isn't likely,' he said . . .
At the end of the day the king's chariot was brought onto
the field . . .
The crowd said nothing could beat those horses.
'My wife is faster,' Crunniuc said . . .

He offered to race her against the horses: she told him she was
pregnant: but he insisted, and the king also insisted.

Her pangs gripped her. She called out to the crowd.
'A mother bore each one of you! Help me. Wait till my
child is born.'
But she couldn't move them.
'Very well,' she said. 'A long lasting evil will come out of
this on the whole of Ulster.'
Then she raced the chariot . . . she gave birth alongside
it . . . As she gave birth she screamed out that all who
heard that scream would suffer from the same pangs for
five days and four nights in their times of greatest
difficulty. This affliction, ever afterward, seized all the
men of Ulster . . .
Only three classes of people were free from the pangs of
Ulster: the young boys of Ulster, the women and
Cuchulainn.
from *The Tain*, translated by Thomas Kinsella

Cuchulainn, one should note, was later to save Ulster because he
had gained the friendship and co-operation of another goddess,
Scathach, who taught him weapon-skills. These legends may not
mean anything to us outside any more: but inside, when Mairead
Farrell told the stories as part of a series of evening entertainment
lectures on celtic and pre-celtic culture, to reaffirm the women's
identity, they seemed to take on an urgent living reality. The
ancient values of truth, justice, logic, science and the arts are still
locked in struggle with the forces of greed and oppression which
would diminish and destroy us all.

On 1 December 1980 Mairead Farrell, Margaret Nugent and Mary Doyle went on hunger strike in Armagh for political status.

> We call upon the Irish people to support us in our stand and we especially call upon our sisters in Ireland and throughout the world to stand and be counted with us in the grave days ahead . . . We are prepared to fast to the death, if necessary, but our love for justice and our country will live for ever.

That is a call that will be understood and identified with by all women all over the world who are victims of state imperialism and personal imperialism.

The Women on Protest in Armagh Jail

Birthdays, when known, have been included. Cards and letters may be sent in, though they are not always allowed through.

From the Belfast Area

Christine Beatty, Ballycastle	12 years
Briege Brownlee, St James (7 August)	8 years
Rosemarie Callaghan, Short Strand (21 July)	5 years
Sile Darragh, Short Strand (4 December)	5 years
Mary Doyle, Greencastle (28 January)	8 years
Mairead Farrell, Andersonstown (3 March)	14 years
Peggy Friel, New Lodge (4 August)	6 years
Maria McClenaghan, Ardoyne (4 May)	5 years
Briege Anne McCaughley, Ballymurphy (1 September)	10 years
Theresa McEvoy, Markets	5 years
Patricia McGarry, Ardoyne (6 November)	10 years
Ellen McGuigan, Lenadoon (23 March)	4 years
Sinead Moore, Lenadoon (17 March)	12 years
Janet Murphy, Bone	5 years
Rosaleen Nolan, Ballymurphy (3 September)	10 years
Mairead Nugent, Andersonstown (28 June)	12 years
Eilis O'Connor, Bone (21 September)	5 years
Katrina Pettigrew, Ballymurphy (20 July)	8 years
Anne Marie Quinn, Ballymurphy (16 May)	12 years

From Derry

Sadie McGilloway (4 October)	8 years
Bernie O'Boyle (11 November)	16 years
Lynn O'Connell (17 February)	8 years

From Other Areas

Anne Bateson, Toombridge (7 July)	20 years
Patricia Craig, Downpatrick (21 January)	8 years
Eileen Morgan, Newry (1 September)	14 years
Dolores O'Neill, Portglenone (7 April)	Life

Women Political Prisoners with Political Status

Dolours Price	Life
Pauline Deery	
Chris Sheerin	

A Short Booklist

Amnesty International, *Report of an Amnesty International Mission to Northern Ireland (November–December 1977)*, Amnesty 1978.

Report of the Committee of Inquiry into Police Interrogation Procedures in Northern Ireland (The Bennett Report), HMSO Cmnd. 7497, 1979.

Tim Pat Coogan, *The IRA*, Fontana.

Tim Pat Coogan, *On the Blanket*, Ward River Press.

Lil Conlon, *Cumann na mBan and the Women of Ireland*, Kilkenny People.

Elizabeth Coxhead, *Daughters of Erin*, Four Square.

Bernadette Devlin, *The Price of My Soul*, Andre Deutsch.

Fr Denis Faul and Fr Raymond Murray, *H Blocks (British Jail for Irish Political Prisoners)*, privately printed.

Michael Farrell, *Northern Ireland: The Orange State*, Pluto Press.

R. M. Fox, *Rebel Irishwomen*, Progress House.

Jack Gale, *Oppression and Revolt in Ireland*, Plough Press.

T. A. Jackson, *Ireland Her Own*, Lawrence & Wishart.

Frank Kitson, *Low Intensity Operations*, Weidenfeld & Nicolsón.

Nell McCafferty, *The Armagh Women*, Dublin Co-op Books.

Eamonn McCann, *War and an Irish Town*, Pluto Press.

John McGuffin, *Internment!*, Anvil.

Margaret MacCurtain and Donncha Ó Corráin (eds.), *Women in Irish Society (The Historical Dimension)*, Arlen House-The Women's Press.

Countess Markievicz, *Prison Letters*, Longmans Green.

O'Dowd, Rolston and Tomlinson, *Northern Ireland: Betweeen Civil Rights and Civil War*, CSE Books.

Prisoners' Aid Committee (eds.) *Irish Voices from English Jails*, published by the editors.

Catherine Rose, *The Female Experience*, Arlen House-The Women's Press.

Peter Taylor, *Beating the Terrorists?*, Penguin Books.

An Phoblacht/Republican News (pub: Belfast/Dublin).

Women Protest for Political Status in Armagh Gaol, pamphlet issued by Women Against Imperialism 1980.

Margaretta D'Arcy

1934   Born.
Father: of Dublin working-class family. Fought in old IRA in War of Independence and on anti-treaty side in Irish civil war. Later posted to London by de Valera government as official in Irish Department of External Affairs. Mother: of Russian Jewish background. Family emigrated from Odessa to East End of London.
Educated and brought up in Dublin. Various schools, including five years in enclosed Dominican convent.

1949–53   Left school and worked in Dublin theatre—influenced by French existentialism and Beckett and Behan.

1953–55   Emigrated to London. Worked in English theatre. Met John Arden. Member of Antony Page's special acting group at Royal Court Theatre in 1958. Came under influence of New Left Review crowd (Doris Lessing, Lindsay Anderson etc.). Member of Irish and British Actors' Equity.

1958-69   Decided to break with authoritarian patriarchal established theatre. Joined Committee of 100 and came under influence of anarchistic-pacifistic community ideologies: used theatre and film to forward these. Worked at community theatre projects in Dublin, Yorkshire, Somerset, New York, London, Scotland. As a result of this work, became further influenced by Black Panther cultural movement, Bread and Puppet Theatre, San Francisco Mime Troupe, Action Cinema in London etc.

1968   Decided to live permanently in Ireland and concentrate energies there because of Civil Rights movement and the revival of the National Question.

1969   Joined Civil Rights in County Galway and made a film for the Land League. Went to India to study non-violent and self-sufficiency movement in rural areas (discovered this to be non-viable in practice); also studied the use of folk theatre in political agitation. Arrested and imprisoned with family in Assam. Gave notice of hunger strike to secure release of my children. (With my husband in the men's jail they had 'political status': but in the women's jail there were no political prisoners—it was also the local madhouse.)

1970　Returned to Ireland and joined official Sinn Fein. Helped to set up theatre, film and newspaper in Galway. Joined Society of Irish Playwrights.

1972　Expelled from official SF (with hundreds of others) because of political disagreements over National Question. Went on strike at Royal Shakespeare Co. with John Arden, as members of Society of Irish Playwrights. First strike ever of playwrights at a British theatre. *Ballygombeen Bequest* withdrawn from 7/84 repertoire because of libel suit.

1973-75　Worked in USA, Canada and community theatre/film projects in Corrandulla, County Galway.

1975　Official Sinn Fein and Irish Transport and General Workers' Union sponsored *Non-Stop Connolly Show* in Liberty Hall, Dublin—the first ever mammoth left-wing cultural statement on Irish stage. Toured Ireland north and south with show.

1976　Formed Galway Theatre Workshop. Presented *Non-Stop Connolly Show* in London.

1977　Toured with Galway Theatre Workshop in Ireland north and south with anti-repression anti-imperialist plays. Some members of group including myself arrested by Gardai in Galway: an attempt made to have us lynched by Fine Gael crowd. Libel case settled. *Pinprick of History*—a play about the Galway Theatre Workshop and Irish repression—presented in London. Attacked by British press for its 'rampant republicanism': also with personal attack on my family for taking part in it.

1978　7/84 present *Vandaleur's Folly*—toured to Belfast. I got arrested for making artistic statement in Ulster Museum in protest against banning of Art for Society exhibitors and H block march. Three weeks among political prisoners in Armagh Jail. Praised by magistrate, fined, and released. Invited to International Writers' Conferences in Norway and Greece.

1979   Arrested with 'Armagh Eleven' on International Women's Day in Armagh. Worked with International Tribunal on Britain's presence in Ireland; Women in Ireland; and Galway Theatre Workshop (opposing EEC elections). Charged with ten others at Armagh: trial postponed three times.

1980   Armagh trial postponed yet again. Trip to New York: sponsored by War Resisters' League and anti-nuclear movement to do theatrical agitation work on H Block and Armagh, culminating in a 30-hour marathon at Washington Square Church: out of which came New York Smash H Block/Armagh Committee and visit of Berrigan brothers to Ireland. Sentenced to prison in my absence in default of paying fine. May 14th—went to Armagh Jail (discovered Breige Anne McCaughley, a cellmate, had seen Galway Theatre Workshop perform in Belfast and had enjoyed it!). August 14th—released.

Margaretta D'Arcy and John Arden

In the last ten years most of Margaretta D'Arcy and John Arden's plays have been on the subject of Ireland—controversial and often censored for dealing directly with sensitive political subjects. Writing in *New Society*, Albert Hunt said of the *Non-Stop Connolly Show*: '. . . I'm uncomfortably aware that I failed to report the major theatrical development in Britain in the 1970s, one which has been very largely ignored by theatre managements and by most critics (including myself).'

In these censorious circumstances, the availability of D'Arcy/Arden's Irish plays in print is particularly important.

The Non-Stop Connolly Show
A Dramatic Cycle of Continuous Struggle in Six Parts

In Easter 1976 Liberty Hall in Dublin saw the world premier of a remarkable 24 hour show chronicling the career of James Connolly, Ireland's greatest revolutionary, from his birth in Edinburgh through his political maturation in Ireland and America to his last moments in front of a British firing squad after the abortive uprising of 1916. Superb history, superb politics, superb drama. 'Poetic powers flash through the dialogue in every sequence.' *The Times*

Part 1: Boyhood 1868-1889 and Part 2: Apprenticeship 1889-1896
ISBN 0 904383 80 6

Part 3: Professional 1896-1903
ISBN 0 904383 81 4

Part 4: The New World 1903-1910
ISBN 0 904383 82 2

Part 5: The Great Lockout 1910-1914
ISBN 0 904383 83 0

Part 6: World War and the Rising 1914-1916
ISBN 0 904383 84 9

Margaretta D'Arcy and John Arden

The Little Gray Home in the West

A young Irish trade union organiser returns home from Manchester for his father's funeral in the West of Ireland: only to find himself involved in a train of events that leads him over the Northern Irish Border to his terrifying death at the hands of the 'security forces'. Culminating in the savage confusion of 1971, the year of internment, *The Little Gray Home in the West* analyses many strands, economic and social as well as political, in the tangled web of the still continuing Irish conflict.

The authors present their story as a fast-moving satirical melodrama, black and hilarious by turns.

ISBN 0 86104 221 2

Geoffrey Bell

The Protestants of Ulster

"An insider's analysis which does undoubtedly capture something of the flavour of that beleaguered community". *Times Literary Supplement*

0 904383 08 3 paperback

Eamonn McCann

War and an Irish Town

"If you read no other book on modern Ireland, you should read this." *New Society*

0 86104 302 2 paperback

Michael Farrell

Northern Ireland: The Orange State

". . . the research is meticulous and his book will be of great value to all those attempting to understand what is happening in Northern Ireland today." *Books and Bookmen*

0 86104 300 6 paperback
0 904383 14 8 hardback

Bernard Ransom

Connolly's Marxism

". . . a very valuable and provocative work." *Irish Press*

0 86104 308 1